In
Black
and
White

In Black and White

A Young Barrister's Story of Race and Class in a Broken Justice System

ALEXANDRA WILSON

ENDEAVOUR

An Hachette UK Company
www.hachette.co.uk

First published in Great Britain in 2020 by Endeavour,
an imprint of
Octopus Publishing Group Ltd
Carmelite House, 50 Victoria Embankment
London EC4Y 0DZ
www.octopusbooks.co.uk

ISBN 978-1-91306-828-8 (Hardback)
ISBN 978-1-91306-829-5 (Paperback)

A CIP catalogue record for this book is available
from the British Library.

Printed and bound in the United Kingdom

10 9 8 7 6 5 4 3 2 1

Some names and descriptions have been changed
to protect identities.

For my family, who have supported me through everything
and have always believed in me.
And in loving memory of my friend 'K',
my Uncle Pat and my Aunty Sue.

Contents

Note to Readers

To protect both privacy and confidentiality, I have made changes to each of the cases in this book. Nobody's real name has been used. I do not name any courts or give the real names of other barristers or any members of the judiciary. I do not identify the locations where any alleged crimes or incidents have taken place.

As expected, some criminal cases that I observed during pupillage were reported in the news. In these few cases, I only write as an outside observer, similar to any member of the public who attends court.

Whilst adult criminal cases are heard in open courtrooms (where the public can attend), family and youth court proceedings are conducted in private. Any out-of-court discussions between a client and their legal representative are also confidential. These deserve additional disguise to ensure further anonymity.

As any criminal or family practitioner will confirm, no client is ever the same but there are issues that may feel familiar throughout this book. It is important, for a number of reasons, to preserve the confidentiality of discussions that took place between me, my colleagues and our respective clients. I have altered details and/or combined features of several cases so that there is no danger of any individual being identifiable to anyone other than themselves.

1
My Story

It was slowly darkening outside. I switched on my desk lamp and turned to the next page of my maths textbook. I was starting to feel sleepy but I'd promised myself that I would finish the questions in this chapter before I went to bed. The numbers were blurring into one lump of black ink. I took a sip of my lukewarm mocha, hoping that the caffeine might give me some energy. My A level exams were only a few weeks away and this was the last stretch.

Question 56.

I glanced at the equation and began to pencil my workings into my notebook.

'Alexandra, I need to speak to you.'

Alexandra?

The formal version of my name floated past.

My thoughts had been interrupted. I had just settled back into my revision and my dad wanted to speak to me now, of all times?

'Err…yes, Dad?'

'Alexandra…'

His repetition of my full name made me nervous. My dad

never called me Alexandra. Even when I was in trouble my name was shortened to the two-syllable 'Alex'. I figured Alexandra was a bit of a mouthful when you wanted to tell someone off. My dad had learned from his Jamaican parents that telling a child off is all about maintaining control of the situation.

He slowly stepped into my room and sat on the bed next to my desk. 'Alex. I need to speak to you.' His voice was softer this time.

I looked up from my book and turned to face him. His eyes seemed swollen. In that brief moment I thought I could see tears in his eyes. I swivelled my chair to face him.

'Al—' Dad's voice broke mid-sentence.

I turned off my CD player and closed my notebook. I clearly wasn't going to finish these questions tonight. Silence engulfed the room. My dad's troubled expression unsettled me.

'Alex, I have just had a call from Aunty Beth. Ayo has been killed.'

My notebook dropped from my hands onto the wooden floor in one sudden action. My dad's face melted into a hazy blur as tears began to fill my eyes.

Ayo had been out that day with a friend. They had been playing football and were on their way to see his friend's aunt. Finding themselves in an unfamiliar area, they were chased into a cul-de-sac by two boys, both of whom were on the prowl for rival gang members. The boys' friend had been stabbed earlier that day; they believed by an opposing gang. They wanted to avenge his death.

Ayo was not in a gang. He was just an unfamiliar face to these boys. He was a black teenage boy in the wrong place at the wrong time. His friend managed to escape from the cul-de-sac. Ayo was not so fortunate. He was caught by the boys. Despite pleading with them that he was not from the area, he was stabbed over 14 times before being left for dead. Paramedics pronounced him dead at the scene. He was just 17 years old.

The truth is, I cannot remember my dad telling this to me but I was left with the vivid mental image of Ayo being stabbed multiple times and left on the ground to die.

In the days that followed, newspaper websites published chilling CCTV footage of Ayo being chased into the cul-de-sac. The footage is haunting.

Ayo's funeral was devastating. The order of service included an array of pictures taken throughout his short life. In bold lettering at the bottom it stated: '17 years old'. This, and the presence of so many young people at the funeral, brought home that his life had been taken too soon. Family and friends had t-shirts made commemorating his life.

* * *

Ayo's death changed me.

I wanted answers. I couldn't understand why Ayo's life had been taken so casually. These boys didn't know him, they had never met him before, but had killed him within minutes.

The assumptions made by law enforcement institutions about black boys being affiliated with gangs seem to have seeped into every part of society. In February 2012, the Metropolitan Police established a 'gangs violence matrix', a data collection and risk assessment tool to track and assess the risk of violence posed by London's allegedly 'known gang members'. By July 2016, 78 per cent of people on the matrix were black (only 13 per cent were white and 9 per cent other ethnic minority groups) and 90 per cent were male. An Amnesty International report on the gangs violence matrix highlighted that many of the indicators used by the Metropolitan Police to identify members of gangs, 'simply reflect elements of urban youth culture and identity that have nothing to do with serious crime'.[1] The police are operating on inaccurate and prejudiced stereotypes, which are then exacerbated by biased media reports. It is hardly surprising that young people are wrongly identifying rival gang members when the police force are doing so too.

A lot of the rhetoric around knife crime in the UK suggests that the victims are affiliated with gangs. It is

---

[1] 'Trapped in the Matrix', report by Amnesty International, https://www.amnesty.org.uk/trapped-gangs-matrix

assumed that the only reason a young black male would be stabbed is because he is part of a gang. Ayo was never part of a gang and yet his life was stolen.

We do not blame a bank when it is robbed. We do not blame a child when they are abused. We should not blame victims of knife crime when they are seriously harmed, or even killed. The victims of knife violence are not always gang members. Ayo's death showed me that innocent young people can be caught up in gang violence merely because of their skin colour. He was a young black boy in the wrong place at the wrong time.

Ayo was murdered in London, less than an hour from where he lived. I couldn't help but question: would the boys who killed him have acted the same way if Ayo had been white? Both Ayo and his friend were black and there was nothing more that would have led the boys to assume they were part of a rival gang. They were not wearing any clothes to suggest gang affiliation; they were not hanging around in a group with known gang members; they were not armed with any weapons. To those boys, Ayo was just another black boy who they didn't know and who they took for members of a rival gang in that area of London.

So, would Ayo have still been killed if he had been white? It is clear that black victims in London are overrepresented in homicides.[2] And this isn't just in London – across England and Wales black children in particular are disproportionately at risk of being killed compared to other children.[3]

Of course, knife crime is not an issue that only affects the black community, despite the media's focus on black-on-black youth knife crime. Knife crime is also prevalent in areas that are almost exclusively white. The first knife offence I knew of was when a white boy brought a knife into my primary school. My classmate had something in common with many others who commit knife crime offences: he was living in poverty and had become involved in criminal activity outside of school. Most of the areas where there are high levels of violent offending are also the most deprived. Figures show that three-quarters of the boroughs in London with the

---

[2] There were a total of 377 homicides in London where the ethnicity of the victim was recorded between 2015 and 2018. The highest number of homicide victims was among black people (160 or 42 per cent). There were 152 (40 per cent) white victims, 41 (11 per cent) Asian victims and 24 (or 6 per cent) victims of another ethnicity. https://assets.publishing.service.gov.uk/government/uploads/system/uploads/attachment_data/file/849200/statistics-on-race-and-the-cjs-2018.pdf

[3] Across all ethnic groups, victims who were under 18 made up a minority of victims (11 per cent). At a group level this percentage was similar for the white (11 per cent), Asian (10 per cent) and 'other' (12 per cent) ethnic groups. However, in the black ethnic group, child victims accounted for 17 per cent of all homicides. Victims from the black ethnic group accounted for 20 per cent of all child victims compared to 12 per cent of adult victims. https://assets.publishing.service.gov.uk/government/uploads/system/uploads/attachment_data/file/849200/statistics-on-race-and-the-cjs-2018.pdf

highest levels of violent offending are also in the top ten most deprived, while the same boroughs also have higher proportions of children and youths under 20 living in poverty than the London average.[4] The disproportionate number of black victims correlates with the fact that black people are more likely than any other ethnic group to live in the most deprived areas.[5]

Knife crime is no distant academic issue for me. It's a reality that cruelly affected me and my family. Poverty disproportionately affects the black community and the result is that black people, like Ayo, are losing their lives, and the perpetrators often seem to be young boys themselves. There are people like me: my age, my race, who grew up in big cities, who are either losing their lives or losing their freedom to lengthy prison sentences.

After Ayo's death, I began to develop an interest in similar cases. I was trying to find an explanation as to what had happened, senseless though it was. Over the next few years, I started to follow reported cases as they appeared in the news. The cases were fascinating and I developed

---

[4] https://www.london.gov.uk/press-releases/mayoral/full-links-between-poverty-and-violent-crime

[5] Among the broad ethnic groups, black people were most likely to live in the most deprived neighbourhoods, followed by Asian people – 19.6 per cent and 17.1 per cent of these groups lived in the most deprived 10 per cent of neighbourhoods. https://www.ethnicity-facts-figures.service.gov.uk/uk-population-by-ethnicity/demographics/people-living-in-deprived-neighbourhoods/latest

an interest in the law underpinning the court's decisions. I visited criminal courts on my days off from sixth form college to watch the trials, particularly at the Old Bailey where they would decide the most serious cases. In sentencing hearings, I would listen to the prosecutor reel off a long list of previous convictions and give details of the significant amount of time that many defendants had spent in care, in pupil referral units (alternative schools for children who are excluded from mainstream education) and often young offender institutions as children. Some of the previous crimes were serious but many were petty and I wondered how different their lives might have been had they not been involved in the criminal justice system from such an early age.

A close family member works in a pupil referral unit and sees the daily challenges that so many of these children who have been rejected by mainstream education face. He was threatened by a 13-year-old student and the police, taking the threat seriously, found that the student had brought a 4-inch blade into school that morning and had hidden it just outside the school gate. It was terrifying to think that at just 13 years old he had already made choices that could have meant taking someone's life and would have put him in prison for a long time.

Later, when I became a law student, I would sit among defendants' and victims' families in the waiting area at court. I heard parents arguing with court staff about having to wait all morning and the struggle to find childcare. I saw young people with obvious learning and behavioural difficulties who were not getting the support they needed.

Many of these families were black or from an ethnic minority background but that diversity was not reflected in the people representing them. There seemed to be such a disconnect when a white, male barrister with an upper-class accent approached these families. The barrister would often tower over the family, who were sitting down in the crowded public waiting area because the courts rarely have enough rooms for families to have a private conference. I saw family members nodding along to the pace of the barrister's speech, until he turned his back and they would then try to decipher what they had just been told. The barrister often left as quickly as he had arrived, leaving no room for questions.

Other families would try to talk at the barrister, expressing their frustrations with a system that was against them from the start. I remember seeing a single mother crying in front of her barrister, explaining that she worked every hour she could in order to provide a roof over her child's head and to ensure that he had enough food to eat. She said that she wasn't able to monitor his behaviour at all times because she had to work double shifts and she couldn't afford alternative childcare. Her other son had been killed just last year and she didn't understand how her son in court had been caught up in the same offending behaviour. I could see the barrister nodding along apparently sympathetically. Eventually he said: 'Don't worry, you will be able to go and visit him in prison.'

Unsurprisingly this didn't reassure the mother, who became hysterical. I could see the barrister awkwardly gazing around. We locked eyes for a brief second. He apologised to the mother and walked away. It was obvious that he had no idea what this woman was going through. His experiences were so far removed from hers.

It was watching moments like this that made me realise how important diversity is in the legal profession. I wanted to be able to give people a voice and be instrumental in changing the path of their lives. There are so many young people drawn into this system who are struggling to find their way out. I decided I wanted to be a barrister.

Ayo's life has motivated me every single time things have got hard. His dreams and ambitions were stolen from him. Honouring my own dreams and ambitions, in his memory, felt like the very least I could do.

* * *

Five years after Ayo's death, at just 22 years old, I received an offer for pupillage – the traineeship to become a qualified barrister. I had been reminded by everyone in and outside of the profession how difficult it was to obtain a pupillage.[6] Every time I did work experience (also known as a 'mini-pupillage') I was kindly reassured that it can take many years for a barrister to obtain pupillage and that I should prepare myself for that.

The thought of this scared me as the one-year course cost nearly as much as my entire undergraduate degree, so I applied for pupillage whilst studying for my graduate diploma in law (GDL) – the law conversion course. Managing my time whilst studying for the GDL full time had been tough. I was undertaking numerous mini-pupillages and working part-time at a local school to fund my studies.

I knew that the BPTC course would be just as intense and twice as expensive. It dawned on me that working part time would not be enough so I applied for a scholarship from my Inn of Court, Middle Temple. I

---

[6] Pupillage is competitive because of the number of applicants per place. There are somewhere between 400 and 500 pupillage places available each year. In 2017/18, 1,619 students enrolled on the Bar Professional Training Course. Once the BPTC has been completed, the qualification is usually only valid for five years so the candidate usually must find pupillage in that time. Each year a candidate is not only competing with their peers but also those who have successfully completed the course in previous years but have not yet obtained pupillage. https://www.barstandardsboard.org.uk/uploads/assets/7a20eb3e-b152-4777-9e821417bf596eed/bptckeystatisticsreport2019.pdf

was overwhelmed when I received the news that I would be starting my training a year later and that I had been awarded the most prestigious scholarship at Middle Temple: the Queen's Scholarship. The scholarship and a bursary from my law school (BPP) covered the entire cost of my fees. When you take the BPTC course, you learn everything from drafting legal documents to courtroom advocacy in under a year. It felt very intense. I was studying full time and trying, as many aspiring barristers do, to balance this studying with voluntary work. I visited homeless shelters, schools and prisons with a charity called Street Law, which aims to help educate the public about their rights and responsibilities in law. At this point, though, I had studying fatigue. I had completed my three-year degree (in politics, philosophy and economics, or PPE), my one-year law conversion course and was now continuing my studies to obtain this essential barrister qualification.

In the lead up to my exams I was asked to help out with a mock trial. This is a demonstration of how a case is tried, and this particular project involved a real judge and barristers conducting a mock criminal trial with professional actors in a courtroom at the Royal Courts of Justice. The trial would be based on a genuine criminal case. It was being organised by two charities, Urban Lawyers and Lawyers in the Soup Kitchen, in partnership with the National Justice Museum and some school-aged students were invited to get involved as part of a wider initiative to help educate young people about the criminal justice system and, in particular, the principle of 'joint enterprise law'.[7]

The barrister leading the mock trial introduced the exercise and explained what would be happening. The students were invited to examine the evidence and the barrister handed out the papers. On the front page, in capital letters, I saw the now familiar capital 'R', representing the prosecution in the name of Regina (the Queen). Regina *versus* the defendants. I glanced further down the page to read the defendants' names. My eyes immediately stopped. I recognised the names.

It couldn't be them. I told myself that it was virtually impossible that his case would have been selected for this mock trial. But I could feel a stone growing in my throat. I tried to take deep breaths. I turned to the next page.

The letters swam across the paper. I scanned the page hoping for a break in the black squiggles. One word stood out to me. It looked like it had been carved into this A4

---

[7] Under this principle, a person involved in a criminal activity with others can be held jointly criminally liable for any further crimes that result from that initial criminal activity, even if they don't personally commit the further crime. For example, if person A and person B commit a robbery together but, during the robbery, person B decides to then shoot someone and kills them, person A could be held jointly criminally liable for the shooting.

sheet of paper and painted in the same red paint used to coat the famous English post-boxes.

Ayo.

The 'high profile murder case' that had been chosen for use as a tool to educate young people was Ayo's. Salty tears trickled down my face as I rushed to use the bathroom.

I returned to the mock trial a few minutes later. The next few hours crawled by.

I tried to stay focused as the police constable gave his evidence.

'Could you walk us through what happened when you arrived at the scene?' the prosecutor began.

The police officer answered calmly: 'When we arrived, the paramedics were already attending to the person I now know to be Ayo.'

Hearing his name spoken aloud gave me the shivers.

The police officer watched everyone's pens as they scribbled a note and then continued: 'We were told that he had suffered multiple wounds to the back. The paramedics were moving him to the ambulance.'

People continued to scrawl notes in their notepads. I sat still, waiting for what I knew was coming next.

'We heard later that day that he died from his wounds before he reached the hospital.'

I felt the tears collecting in my eyes. I lowered my head and tried to focus on the patterns in the wooden desks.

The prosecutor turned to question the pathologist. The only words I remembered hearing were: 'The deceased would not have lived longer than five minutes.'

New case law on joint enterprise had come into force a few years after Ayo's death. In the past, a person could be convicted of murder without personally intending to kill or cause serious harm themselves. All the jury had to be sure of was that the person could have *foreseen* that serious harm or death would be caused (which is much easier for the prosecution to prove). For example, if you went out with a friend and they ended up killing someone, provided the jury were sure that you could have foreseen that the your friend was going to cause serious harm, then you would also be found guilty of murder.

The change in the law means that you can only be convicted of murder if you also have what's called 'the mental element' – that is, if you intend to kill or cause serious harm. In other words, you can no longer be found guilty of murder merely for *foreseeing* that serious harm or death would be caused.

The trial moved onto the defence case. The actor playing the second defendant embraced the role wholeheartedly. The defence barrister questioned him slowly and thoughtfully.

'Why did you follow the boys?'

'They started to run when they saw us and I thought it

was funny. We started to run after them and I was asking why they were running.'

'Where did they go?'

'They ran into a cul-de-sac. I only saw one of them and he was trying to jump over the wall. Then X went over and started attacking him.' (He referred to the main defendant as 'X', as he refused to identify his friend as the murderer.)

'How did he attack him?'

'He was stabbing him. I was shocked.'

'Why were you shocked?'

'I didn't know he had brought the knives out of the taxi.'

He claimed that X had bought knives for 'protection' earlier that day. However, he said that he had no idea that X had carried the knives out of the taxi with him and so when they approached Ayo and his friend, he didn't know X had a knife. He said he panicked when he saw X attack Ayo. He described himself as being in a trance. X asked him to follow him back to the taxi and he did. He said he didn't know what to do.

'I knew if the police came, they would arrest me. I don't trust the police. I don't trust the system.'

In the real trial, both defendants were convicted. They both faced murder sentences for taking Ayo's life. In the mock trial, one of the defendants was acquitted. The co-defendant was acquited because, according to the new joint enterprise law, the second defendant could not be found guilty of murder; he did not have the requisite intention to cause serious harm to or kill Ayo.

This was difficult to process. I knew that this was not the real case. I knew that it had no bearing on the two boys that were already in prison for murdering Ayo, but a part of me felt that this mock trial had undermined the seriousness of their offences.

But, while it was painful to watch, the unlikely coincidence of Ayo's case being used for this mock trial confirmed my belief that I should pursue a career at the Bar. It felt like Ayo's blessing.

* * *

My parents told anyone who would listen that their daughter was about to become a barrister. My friends and my family sent cards and messages expressing their pride. My extended family live by the mantra that if one of us is doing well, we are all doing well. But not everyone was proud. Some of my family were baffled.

'Cuz, how can you do it? How can you prosecute our brothers and sisters? Don't you feel guilty putting another black person in prison?'

My cousin looked genuinely disappointed in me. He could not understand why a black person, or anyone of black heritage, would want to be part of a system that imprisoned more black people than any other race.

His questions were fair given that the criminal justice system disproportionately affects black people. My cousin wasn't the only person to question me about my decision. My brothers, uncles, other male cousins and male friends were sceptical about me being part of a system that they all suffered under. All of them had been stopped by the police at some point, which is unsurprising given that black people are more than seven times more likely to be stopped and searched than white people and almost four times more likely to be arrested.[8] Discriminatory policing has led to a strained relationship between much of the black community and the police. The Stephen Lawrence Inquiry confirmed what many black people had been saying for years: there is institutional racism within the police.

The problem with my cousin's question is that it is loaded with the assumption that the problems cannot be solved. I was – and still am - convinced that they can, and I want to be a part of making these changes happen. I am a strong believer that the best way to change something

---

[8] The rate of stop and search for black people in the UK is 38 per 1,000 people. This compares to just 4 per 1,000 white people. https://www.ethnicity-facts-figures. service.gov.uk/crime-justice-and-the-law/policing/stop-and-search/latest#by-ethnicity. Black and mixed-race defendants have the 'highest number of prosecutions', which may be a result of the disproportionate number of arrests, or it may indicate bias in charging decisions. Black people receive the longest average custodial sentence lengths. And there are more black and mixed- race individuals in prison compared to other ethnicities. https://www.cps.gov.uk/ publication/code-crown-prosecutors https://assets.publishing.service.gov.uk/ government/uploads/system/uploads/ attachment_data/file/663376/race-cjs- 2016-infographic.pdf.

is from the inside. I see value in prosecution and defence work and I wanted to do both. Prosecuting people who commit crimes is just as important as defending them. To live in a safe society, the rules that protect us all need to be enforced. When people commit serious crimes, there needs to be a way of preventing them from causing further harm to others. Equally, it's important for people who are accused of crimes to be properly represented in proceedings that are likely to change their lives.

My cousin wasn't convinced. He scrunched up his nose and narrowed his eyes. I knew he wasn't finished and I sat there awkwardly waiting for his next question.

'Alex, are you going to fit in?'

I interlocked my fingers and took a deep breath. I sat still for a moment and thought about my answer.

I knew I wouldn't blend in at the Bar but I hoped I would be welcomed. However, there had, in truth, already been many moments in which I'd begun to doubt whether this really was the career for me.

In the long summer after completing the Bar Professional Training Course I'd continued my court visits. One weekday morning, I was waiting outside the courtroom in the public waiting area as I always did. I was dressed smartly: a black knee-length work dress and a black blazer. I convinced myself that if I looked 'the part' maybe I would be seen as a real barrister.

The courtroom usher approached me, and said: 'You must be the defendant? Follow me.'

This wasn't the first time it had happened and it certainly wasn't the last. I was dressed exactly as every other barrister waiting around at court that day and none of them had been taken for the defendant. The only difference between me and them was the colour of my skin.

I'll never forget when I approached a barrister to tell him how interesting it had been to watch his case. It was the end of the day and he was clearly eager to draw the conversation to a close. I mentioned that I was an aspiring barrister and he smiled sympathetically. He reminded me that pupillage is incredibly difficult and that I could help people in other ways. When I told him that I had pupillage and was starting in a few months' time, his jaw dropped.

'Really? You? People like you usually find it very difficult to get pupillage, so well done.'

His shock was obvious but his congratulations seemed genuine. Who were 'people like me'? His reaction was not unusual; most people I meet are shocked when I tell them that I am a barrister. This doesn't surprise me given that every time I attend court, the vast majority of barristers and judges are white, older, male and have been privately educated.

I'm a woman. I am mixed-race. I grew up in East London and Essex. I am not posh but I'm not going to let anyone tell me that the Bar isn't for 'people like me'.

This is my story.

2

First Day in Court

My grandma and I grinned at each other as we stood outside the legal dress shop. Today was a big day; we were buying my wig and gown. I was about to look like a real barrister! We had visited one of the oldest tailors in London, which was nearly 300 years old and specialised in legal dress. The name of the shop was engraved into its glass window in gold handwriting. I had never seen so much polished, dark wood.

We stepped inside and were greeted with polite smiles as the shop assistant asked what we were looking for. My grandma couldn't contain her pride, she exclaimed: 'My granddaughter has just qualified as a barrister and she's starting pupillage, we need to get her a wig and gown!' She was beaming.

We were taken to the back of the store, which added to the enchantment of the experience, and I was asked to stand in front of a tall glass mirror whilst my measurements were taken. The tailor disappeared momentarily and my grandma and I tiptoed around, looking at the old wig tins and wigs decorating the shelves and walls. The tailor returned and I slipped back into position in front of the grand mirror. First the gown was draped over my shoulders as I pushed my arms through the armholes like an eagle spreading her wings. I twirled in front of the mirror and the gown flew up behind me like a cape.

I could hear the rustling as the wig was removed from the box. I stared back at my own reflection, waiting patiently for the curled grey hair to be placed on my head. Slowly the wig was lifted above me and I could see the silver hair sparkle in the light above. It was lowered onto my head and it fitted snugly. From the corner of my eye I could see a tear trickle down my grandmother's cheek.

The woman standing in front of me looked so elegant and composed. She looked like she could take on the world. I wanted to be the woman in the mirror.

However, it's worth noting at this point that the trip to the legal dress shop was not just emotional, it was expensive! To buy a wig and gown – the uniform I would be required to wear in the Crown Court – costs almost £1,000. It's worrying that these items are still so expensive. It is yet another financial barrier to pursuing a career at the Bar.

My grandmother bought me a beautiful dark blue bag to keep my legal dress in, which I had engraved with my initials. Then, there was the wig tin. I was in two minds about this because I think it is absurd to spend £300 on a tin to store your wig in, but it was so beautiful and would be engraved with my full name. I figured I would only ever need one tin, so in 30 years' time it will have worked out at just £10 a year, and if I'm still working in 60 years' time, just £5. My simple maths justified it in my head and clearly my grandmother thought so too as she decided to buy me one of the personalised tins. I will cherish it forever.

* * *

The first day of pupillage finally arrived. I felt as though everything was aligning for this huge moment. Pupillage – our apprenticeship year – is split into two equal parts, and I had been told that it would feel like a 12-month interview, which terrified me.

The first six months would be spent shadowing my supervisors in court. Outside of court, I would be undertaking legal research and drafting legal documents for other members of chambers.[1] I would also be doing advocacy training with my Inn of Court. There are four Inns of Court: Middle Temple, Inner Temple, Gray's Inn and Lincoln's Inn and all students must join one before they start their training. The Inns are essentially professional associations, and they play a crucial role in legal education

---

[1] Barristers work with each other in unincorporated associations to share costs such as administration and clerking. These associations are known as chambers. 'Chambers' can also be used to describe the office building where those barristers and their clerks are based.

for barristers and students. They also hold exclusive rights of admission to the Bar, which is referred to as our 'call to the Bar' and occurs once you have completed the Bar Professional Training Course.

The second six months of my pupillage, which did not seem very far away, would consist of me representing my own clients. I would be able to accept professional instructions from solicitors to represent their clients in court, which meant that I would be sent my own cases to do. Solicitors are responsible for the majority of the client's case preparation out of court, whereas barristers usually represent the client in court. Whilst the professions are separate, there is some overlap and a lot of our work is dependent on the relationships we build with the solicitors that instruct us.

Providing I completed the first six months of training to a satisfactory standard, I would be granted the right to do my own cases (without any supervision or assistance) in the second six months. Although like most barristers I would be self-employed, I learned that the clerks in my chambers would manage my diary and negotiate and liaise with solicitors on my behalf and ensure that I was paid.

I had worked so hard for this moment. I had studied for five years since leaving school and had undertaken too many weeks of unpaid work experience. The pupillage application process had been arduous, involving countless written applications, many rounds of interviews and numerous advocacy exercises. It was exhausting. I knew I was one of the few people who had obtained pupillage on the first attempt – many had to go through the process at least twice. One interview stood out to me more than the others. I was asked about why I wanted to be a barrister. When I explained what had happened to Ayo, the interviewer looked so awkward and shuffled in her seat uncomfortably. I felt so embarrassed and decided not to bring up his story in a professional situation again, which felt like a betrayal of Ayo's memory.

On the eve of my first day, I packed my huge Criminal Law Practice book – better known as *Blackstone's* – into my wheelie trolley alongside at least five pairs of tights (just in case!), emergency sanitary items, notepads, a pencil case and my laptop with the all-important charger. I'd made sure to close every possible application on my laptop before packing it into my bag. I was terrified that I would open my laptop and the reality TV episode that I had been watching would echo around a silent courtroom.

As many parents do the night before their children start school, I laid out my clothes for the next day. My shirt was a crisp white and shone brightly against my black suit. My shoes were ready: a pair of heels and a pair of flats, as I hadn't quite made my mind up about which I would be wearing. I set out my underwear, my tights and even my hairband. I physically couldn't have been more prepared, yet I felt entirely unprepared for the journey I was about to embark on.

I reflected back on the questions from my cousin. Was I going to fit in? I wasn't like other barristers. I could dress up and play the part but I worried that people would see through the facade. Would I be able to do it? The thought of being solely responsible for someone's liberty was daunting. In just six months, my words could affect whether someone would be kept in custody or granted bail while awaiting their trial. My advocacy might affect whether someone would get the court's protection from their abusive ex-partner or whether a parent was able to see their child. Six months felt incredibly soon.

I knew pupillage was going to be hard work – mainly because I had heard numerous horror stories about people not sleeping, becoming ill and having breakdowns during their pupillage year. I understood the basic format, in so far as I knew that I would be shadowing a senior barrister for the first six months, but I had very limited details of anything else. I had been given a start date and, the Friday before I started, I was given the name and email address of my first supervisor. I had no idea what to expect.

I woke up bright and early on my first day of pupillage. My alarm was set for 6am but at 4.45am I was awake and bouncing out of bed. With a wheeled suitcase bigger than me and a mostly empty handbag on my shoulder to 'look the part', I set off two hours earlier than I needed to, just to make sure I was there on time for the first day of pupillage.

I arrived at the designated Crown Court, surprised at my ability to have found it so easily, with no delays to my journey. I felt pleased but then wondered how I'd now kill the spare two hours I had left. In a local café, I found a small, comfy chair in the corner and plugged in my earphones, setting three alarms to make sure I wasn't too engrossed in Netflix when my supervisor arrived to meet me.

'Hi! You must be Alexandra?'

I stood up instinctively to see the beaming smile from a friendly looking man: my first supervisor.

I had looked him up on LinkedIn and connected in advance to avoid the awkwardness of us not being able to recognise each other. Friends warned me that a lot of people use old pictures on their LinkedIn profile so I was expecting a grey-haired version of the man I'd seen online but his hair was undoubtedly brown. He looked like many of the other barristers who I had already come across: tall, white, smartly dressed in a dark blue suit and clean shaven. His smile was infectious and I felt at ease. I grabbed my bitter black coffee – not realising how addictive this drink would become in the months to come – and shoved my earphones into my pocket. I glanced down at my outfit hoping that I hadn't accidently laddered my tights or caught my dress in my underwear. Thankfully, everything seemed to be OK.

As we walked to court, I studied my passing reflection in the windows of the surrounding shops. I adjusted my dress again and buttoned my jacket, anxious to make a good first impression. I looked up at the sky, silently praying to the universe that my frizzy curly hair hadn't come out of place. I'd practically finished an entire tub of hair gel and hairspray trying to glue my hair neatly to my head that morning and hoped that nature wouldn't defeat my willpower. In my eyes, barristers didn't have frizzy curly hair and on day one of pupillage I was not prepared to be the first.

I'd meticulously studied the case papers that had been sent to me a few days before. This was the sort of case I didn't think I'd see until I'd been doing the job for years. The defendant, his wife and another couple were alleged to have been involved in illegally exporting aeroplane parts to the Middle East and money laundering.

The courtroom was large with pale-lemon coloured walls, which made it hard to work out whether it was intentionally painted yellow or it was once white and had slowly faded. The colour matched the off-white tinge of the barrister's wigs. It was a huge case and there were lots of bodies in the courtroom: four defendants, the judge, the clerk, the usher, the IT technician, eight barristers and a nervous, smiley pupil – me. I glanced around the courtroom, quickly at first and then again, slower this time, taking in the small details of everyone's face. I began to play the game I'd played my whole life: 'spot the black person'.

Spot the black person is a game you are never taught to play, it's like the unspoken 'black nod' when you see another black or mixed-race person at a mostly white event. It's an acknowledgment that you are a minority in the environment and it's a way of bringing some light-hearted humour or ease to a situation you feel uncomfortable in. And I did feel uncomfortable. I worried that people would look at me as the token pupil who had been taken on to boost the Bar's diversity statistics; or even just as a work experience student. I worried that people would think that a mixed-race Essex girl couldn't *really* be a pupil barrister.

These were legitimate worries. Although I didn't experience any confrontation during that first case, there were moments during my training where people weren't subtle in their astonishment at my achievements. I was shadowing a divorce case when a fairly young, white, privately educated female barrister (I looked her up afterwards), opened a conversation with me by saying: 'You *must* be on work experience? How are you finding the law?'

I reassured her that I was a trainee barrister. You could tell she couldn't quite believe her eyes. After a further ten questions I'd clearly passed her authenticity checks and she proceeded to tap away at her mobile phone and ignored me for the rest of the morning.

Of course, I wish it didn't matter what I looked like or where I came from. I wish that I hadn't been bothered by what everyone else in the courtroom looked like that first day on the job. My whole life my parents have tried to instil a strong sense of 'it doesn't matter what everyone else is doing, worry about what you are doing.' But it did matter. When I looked around the courtroom that morning, I couldn't help but feel out of place. It was obvious that no one there looked like me. Everyone was white.

Heading to the advocates' robing room after the trial, I still couldn't see anyone that looked even remotely like me. The robing room sounds a lot more majestic than it is. Most courts have a room for barristers to get changed into their robes and these rooms vary hugely in size. In the Central Criminal Court ('the Old Bailey'), where the most serious crimes in the country are tried, the robing rooms are fairly large and spacious with huge tables for barristers to work at. In other courts around the country the robing room is as big as a toilet cubicle and only one person can use it at a time.

The larger robing rooms are often scattered with old case files (despite the numerous signs warning us not to leave any papers in there) and bits that people have left behind. I have found half-eaten sandwiches, mouldy bananas, broken phone chargers and even someone's dentures. One robing room had a substantial leak so all of the barristers' coats were damp when they returned from their hearings. Another robing room had no working lock for a while so barristers kept having their belongings stolen.

The robing rooms are often divided by gender and in many courts the male robing rooms are larger, which emphasises the historic gender imbalance. I would often blindly follow my male supervisor into male robing rooms. He'd joke that although most men actually wouldn't care, I might not want to see an elderly man strip naked merely to change his shirt collar. I couldn't agree more.

There were two female barristers (out of eight) in that first case I observed during pupillage, and they were both exceptional advocates. One of them was already a big name at the Bar and a Queen's Counsel,[2] and the other was relatively junior but had already represented clients in a number of high-profile cases and was recognised as a star-in-the-making.

The more senior of the two would not be returning to court after that morning. She represented one of the wives in the case – who had initially been charged with money

---

[2] Queen's Counsel ('QC') is an award of excellence for barristers.

laundering – and had successfully had the wife's case dismissed. The case proceeded against the others, leaving just one other female barrister.

At the end of the case, the junior female barrister passed on her contact details and offered to be there if I ever needed her. She said that she had been impressed with how much I had helped with legal research and that my note (which I had helpfully emailed to all of the barristers) had really assisted her in her preparation. Her willingness to take time out of her busy schedule to support another woman whose career was clearly its infancy was admirable. This little act of kindness didn't go unnoticed. It was my first experience of how supportive women are of each other at the Bar and I immediately felt pride in being able to be a part of this profession.

Despite this gesture of solidarity, my first day made me realise how important it is for people like me to be able to see people who look like us in the legal profession. Rather than sticking out like a sore thumb, we need to be able to walk into courtrooms and see an equal balance of women and men, in senior positions as well as junior positions. There should be representatives from all types of ethnic and racial backgrounds that better reflect the public we serve. Feeling like an impostor plagued my memory of an otherwise excellent first day of pupillage.

Impostor syndrome has been defined as the psychological experience of believing that one's accomplishments came about not through genuine ability, but as a result of having been lucky, having worked harder than others, or having manipulated other people's impressions.[3] For me, this materialised as feeling like a 'fraud'. That one day I was going to get found out.

The first time I experienced this feeling was when I changed schools for sixth form. My old secondary school was the local state comprehensive school and there was a large focus on behaviour management as opposed to academic excellence. I have vivid memories of a boy in my class repeatedly being locked in a small cupboard every lesson by the other students.

I had studied hard in order to apply to a grammar school for sixth form. I had high hopes. I thought I'd finally fit in. I'd be somewhere where everyone wanted to learn and I'd be supported. That unfortunately wasn't the case. One of the members of staff in my new sixth form welcomed me to the school by telling me that I might have been the best in my old school but certainly wouldn't be the best there. She intimated that my GCSE results were of a lower standard despite the fact that I'd achieved higher grades than all

---

[3] Clance, P. R. & Imes, S. A. (1978). 'The impostor phenomenon in high achieving women: Dynamics and therapeutic intervention', Psychotherapy: Theory, Research, and Practice, 15, 241–247.

of the students at both schools and they were all from the same awarding bodies.

My form tutor laughed when I said I'd be applying for Oxford University and on parents' evening told my mum that I should be aiming for 'more realistic' universities. My school refused to give me a mock interview to help with my preparation when Oxford offered me an interview, claiming there was no one who had any relevant experience.

Thankfully I was part of a pilot scheme (which is now a full programme) called Target Oxbridge, run by Oxford and Cambridge graduates. It is a free programme that aims to help black African and Caribbean students and students of mixed race with black African and Caribbean heritage increase their chances of getting into the universities of Oxford or Cambridge. They provided mentorship and support in the application process and the leader of the scheme, who was my personal mentor, organised for her friend to provide me with a mock interview when my school refused to. The content of the interview wasn't important; it was all about having that small bit of confidence that the real interview at Oxford wouldn't be my first ever interview.

I passed the interview, achieved the A level grades I'd worked so hard towards and I got into Oxford. And yet again I felt a huge sense of impostor syndrome during my time there. Other students told me I was too working class to be at Oxford and my Essex accent was continually mocked. I was the only black person in my year in college and on one occasion I was told that I *must* play the steel pans because I'm black. I felt out of place and frustrated that I didn't know how to deal with their ignorance.

This experience taught me valuable lessons about impostor syndrome that I brought to the Bar. I learned that there will be people who might try to make you feel uncomfortable or make you feel like you are invading their space. In my first year of training I kept having to remind myself that I am no less welcome at the Bar than anyone else.

Shortly after joining the profession, a senior, male, white barrister took pride in telling me that whilst lower crime rates are 'bad for business', the black community have 'helped us out by killing each other'. He continued to talk about how knife crime was rising and providing more work but, frustratingly for him, the young people being charged were choosing black barristers who he felt were not as good as him. Not only was I struck by how blatantly offensive his comment was, it made me realise he had never imagined that a barrister might have direct experience of losing someone close to them to knife crime. I thought back to my cousin's question of why I was doing this job. It was so clear that the profession needs people like me.

However, as a trainee barrister it can feel as though your ability to call out offensive remarks is limited due to a fear of having a black mark against your name. As a pupil, you are desperate to be taken on as a tenant, which means you are given a permanent place in a chambers as a self-employed barrister and enables you to associate your name with the chambers, sharing the clerking and administration. This decision is made at the end of your pupillage year, so you feel a constant pressure to impress.

I think so much of this would improve if there was greater representation throughout the profession; not just in the pupil intake.[4] Whilst at the entry level diversity has improved considerably, there is more work to be done.

---

[4] The Bar Standards Board's 2018 diversity report revealed that 13.6 percent of pupil barristers compared to 8.1 per cent of QCs are black, Asian and minority ethnic (BAME).

3

How I Defend the Guilty

'Yeah, I've seen the CCTV. Look, I'm going to just deny everything. I'm pleading not guilty.'

It was just days before Christmas but the Crown Court was as busy as ever. I was a few months into my pupillage, shadowing a male junior barrister who was representing a client accused of burgling an office. Mr Mason had a long history of theft and burglary convictions and many of them were from earlier that year. He was on a suspended sentence, which meant that if he pleaded guilty to these latest offences, he was likely to be sentenced for these offences as well as serving (at least some of, if not all of) the sentence given to him on the last occasion. He was looking at an immediate custodial sentence – in other words, he would be going to prison today.

The barrister explained that the evidence was compelling: there was clear CCTV showing a man looking just like Mr Mason entering and leaving the building; there were numerous witnesses who described a man like Mr Mason, and the electronic tablets stolen from the office had been recovered from his home.

'So what are you saying?' Mr Mason asked. His tone was calm.

'I'm just saying, you might want to consider pleading guilty.' The barrister paused and took a deep breath. 'Look, it's your choice, Mr Mason. May I remind you, if you plead guilty your sentence will be reduced, you'll be given credit for your guilty plea.'

Mr Mason laughed, 'Yeah, mate, I know. Up to one third, this isn't my first time in court, you know.'

The barrister unfolded his arms and pushed his laptop screen down. 'Well, it really is your choice, but we don't have much time.'

Mr Mason's tone changed. He became more aggressive and raised his hands as he spoke.

'So what's the point of you being here? I pay you to put my case across. If I say, "I didn't do it", you tell the court that I didn't do it.' He looked furious. He knew the system well and wasn't afraid to demonstrate his knowledge. 'I have bail and I want you to go into court and tell them that I am pleading not guilty. If I change my mind, I can plead guilty after Christmas and still get a decent amount of credit.'

The barrister awkwardly shuffled in his seat. 'OK. Let's go then.' He stood up and both Mr Mason and I followed him out of the conference room and into the courtroom. I sat behind the barrister as Mr Mason was escorted into the secure dock.

The judge saw right through Mr Mason's game plan and asked the barrister whether Mr Mason had properly considered the prosecution evidence. He asked what the issues at trial were and the barrister asserted that Mr Mason disputed that it was him in the CCTV and in the witness descriptions.

The judge began to question the barrister: 'Has Mr Mason seen the CCTV evidence?'

'Yes, Your Honour.'

'Has he seen the CCTV, showing a clear facial image?'

'Yes.'

The barrister reassured the judge that everything had been duly considered and Mr Mason wished to maintain his not guilty plea. The judge expressed surprise that Mr Mason had previously been granted bail but made a note of the fact that Mr Mason was challenging the identification evidence. He set some dates for the prosecution and defence to file and serve the relevant evidence. The next hearing would be in February.

We left the hearing and Mr Mason smiled at us as he walked over to his partner and child.

'I just wanted to be at home this Christmas. I'll change my plea in the new year.'

* * *

Barristers have a duty to the court; we cannot intentionally deceive the court or the jury in presenting our case. I expect that some people imagine a scenario where a defendant spills all to their barrister and then the two collude about what story to give the court to cover the defendant's tracks. But in reality, colluding with a client about what version of events to tell the court is forbidden by our code of conduct. In reality, it is extremely rare that a client will tell you that they are guilty and then be adamant that they are pleading not guilty. As with Mr Mason, the evidence might be overwhelming but a client can still maintain that they are not guilty. Clients will usually tell their barristers whatever story they want them to tell the court.

If a client tells us that they committed a crime, we can still represent them at trial but we must not advance a positive case that they did not commit the offence. In other words, I cannot knowingly mislead the court. I can't accuse the witnesses of lying when I know that they are telling the truth and I can't call my client to give evidence that I know is fictitious. All I can do is 'put the prosecution to proof', which means that I can challenge the prosecution evidence, which might include challenging the admissibility of evidence or addressing the judge on the law. For example, I could cross-examine a witness on any inconsistencies between the evidence she has given orally in court and the written evidence that she gave in her witness statement. I can also make submissions to the court about the evidence not being strong enough to prove my client's guilt. However, I cannot tell the court that he did not commit the offence if I know he did. It's a myth that comes from crime dramas that lawyers help defendants mislead the judge and jury – we are prohibited from doing so.

One of the questions I asked myself before entering this profession was, how I would defend someone that I know is guilty? But in actual fact I don't struggle with the idea of representing people who most likely have done what they are accused of. Everyone deserves representation. No matter how bad the alleged crime or who the person is, it is an essential part of a fair justice system to ensure that everyone is properly represented. It is imperative that there are excellent barristers on both sides.

In a well-functioning society, people should only be convicted if we can be sure of their guilt and should only face a punishment proportionate to the crime. One way to ensure this is for every defendant to have good legal representation, as well as the state being well represented. Some doubt may be cast on how well this theory can be implemented when some defendants are able to pay privately for their representation and can thus pay for the most experienced advocates to represent them in cases that would not warrant an advocate with that level of skill. However, this is largely combatted by the fact that most criminal barristers (even the most experienced) do legal aid work in addition to their privately paying work. This means that for all criminal cases, especially the most serious cases, a defendant will be able to have an advocate of the appropriate level even if they cannot afford to pay for private representation.

I do more defence work but that distribution can vary considerably among criminal barristers. Some only prosecute or only defend, whereas others do a mix, like me. Your chambers can affect the type of work that you do. Some are known for specialising in either prosecution or defence. A real benefit of defence work is that I am able to spend a lot of time with clients. As a prosecutor, the witnesses are not your client, you represent the state.

In family law cases, I represent both applicants and respondents; applicants ask for a court order and respondents either accept or challenge the imposition of an order. For example, I often act for individuals who want the court's protection from an abusive ex-partner or family member by applying for a non-molestation order. And on other occasions, I represent the men and women who contest these protective orders. Similarly, in criminal cases, I prosecute and defend. In domestic abuse cases, in the criminal courts, I have prosecuted alleged perpetrators as well as defending them. It is fascinating to be able to see both sides of a case. Working on both sides enables you to better identify strengths and weaknesses in future cases.

However, in my first few weeks as a pupil barrister, I wasn't faced with the ethical dilemma of representing a guilty client but rather the difficulty of staying focused while taking notes for other barristers all day. As a trainee barrister in my first six months of pupillage, I had no rights of audience. In simple terms, this means that whilst court is sitting you cannot address the judge or the magistrates – you don't have the right to speak in court. This can leave you feeling like a spare part but you do observe what others might miss.

I was instructed to do a noting brief, which involves a pupil or junior barrister attending a trial and keeping a note. The big benefit of this to most pupil barristers is that you can be useful and it gets you noticed. At the end of each day, you are asked to send the detailed note to the barristers in the trial, or barristers in an upcoming trial that would be affected by what's happened in the courtroom you have been sitting in all day. The barristers and the judge in the current trial are appreciative as it helps them to keep a record of everything that has happened and thus helps them to prepare for the next day of questioning. The barristers in the upcoming trial are also grateful to be kept in the loop.

When there are multiple defendants in the same case, a trial is often split into smaller trials. In this particular Crown Court case, there were almost 20 defendants being tried for perverting the course of justice. The defendants were alleged to have been involved in removing electronic tags (used to monitor people who are given a curfew by the court). One of the defendants had the professional tools to remove the tags and a number of the others were accused of using his services to ensure that their tags were removed without setting off an alert so that no one would be any the wiser. There were too many defendants to squeeze into one dock and so a joint trial would be entirely impractical. The trial was therefore split into a number of trials, all to be heard by the same judge, but with different juries.

My wrists ached from furiously taking notes. I hadn't anticipated that note taking would be such an important skill. I began to wish that I'd asked my nail therapist to cut my nails just a tad shorter. I also wished that people would slow down when they spoke. I'd occasionally hear a barrister interrupt the witness to tell them to keep an eye on the judge's pen and to slow down but it wasn't the witnesses I was struggling to keep up with. The judge spoke quickly and I was typing furiously to keep pace.

In the electronic tag trial, all but one of the defendants were convicted. I remember how much I learned about different advocacy styles: there were theatrical barristers who commanded the jury's attention; barristers who would address the jury in a conversational tone, subtly persuading them to find their client not guilty. I was captivated by the casual questions that would lead the witness to one specific answer: the answer the barrister wanted. For the first time, I had seen props being used. The electronic tags were brought in for the jury to see and they were opened and closed with a specialist fitting tool, so that the jury could understand how the offences had been committed. The barristers used these props in questioning the witnesses and the jury seemed to find this a welcome break from the folders of written evidence.

Props can be really helpful to illustrate a point to a jury, who may have little or no background knowledge. For example, on the advocacy course held at the Inns of Court, we had been taught how to use a doll and a model of a pelvis to demonstrate a baby being delivered to show a tribunal how medical injuries had been sustained during childbirth, which is essential for determining whether there had been any medical negligence. In our vulnerable witness advocacy training, we similarly learned that children who may have been the victims of abuse can often use dolls to show where they were injured or where they had been touched.

The prohibition on speaking in the first six months of pupillage proved quite comical one day when the judge in the electronic tag trial asked me a question about what had been said just before lunch. I had the answer right in front of me but I didn't know if I was allowed to say it. My colleagues had emphasised that during our first six months as a pupil we must not speak in court under any circumstances. But now the judge had asked me a direct question and I was staring at her blankly. An explosion of thoughts went through my head: should I write her a note? Or whisper the answer to the closest barrister for him to say it out loud? I knew that this was ridiculous but I didn't want to breach a serious rule.

The judge repeated the question, assuming I hadn't heard her the first time. Was I supposed to stand up to address her, as the barristers did, even though I wasn't allowed to speak? I decided to half stand up and whisper my answer, which felt less like a breach than standing up properly and communicating clearly, but in reality must have been annoying.

The judge looked confused and I panicked. I repeated my answer loudly and clearly. She nodded and returned to addressing the barristers. There were no fireworks and the Bar Standards Board didn't march in to take me away. I had spoken in court and everything was OK.

* * *

I turned up one cold, winter Monday morning at the

Crown Court for the noting brief. My laptop was charged and I was ready to attack my keyboard at the speed of light. One of the barristers I'd got to know over the past few weeks followed me into the robing room and apologised that I had arrived so early when I wasn't needed until the afternoon. He had asked the judge for time to consider an important legal issue connected to his case so court wouldn't be sitting until 2pm. It was 9.30am so I called my supervisor who recommended observing another case. It made sense. This court wasn't particularly close to the rest of civilisation and I would still be needed in the afternoon.

I asked the court ushers what looked interesting and ended up watching a grievous bodily harm (GBH) trial with two co-defendants. The men were an odd pair: one was short and stocky with a bald head. His features were all squished into the middle of his face and his eyebrows stood out. The other man was tall and skinny with an unremarkable face and plain brown hair.

I watched the tall man tell his story, noticing how often he turned to the shorter stocky man. The judge was clearly distracted by this behaviour and asked him to stay focused on giving his evidence to the jury, no one else. Every time he was asked a difficult question he would turn and look at his co-defendant before answering. He had a slight stutter and it worsened as his evidence progressed.

The lunch break came and the judge gave everyone

an hour to stretch their legs, take a comfort break and eat some food. The judge emphasised that the defendant must not talk to anyone about his evidence as he was still in the middle of giving evidence to the court. I was hungry; my morning rush meant that I'd skipped breakfast. I headed to the canteen hoping that it would not take the entire hour to get to the front of the long lunch queue. As I stood there I couldn't help but overhear the conversation behind me. A man was talking to someone about his evidence:

'How did I sound? Do you think they believed me?'

Another person confirmed that he sounded good and the first speaker continued: 'Obviously, I don't want the jury to think that…' his voice was drowned out as the café assistant asked for my order. I placed my order and could hear the conversation continue; it began to sound increasingly familiar. The judge had explicitly warned the co-defendant that he should not be talking about his evidence. I tried to focus on the slowly shortening queue in front of me.

'Excuse me miss, are you a lawyer or a police officer?'

I turned to see that I did not recognise the two males behind me. One of them looked similar to the tall man but he had longer hair and piercing eyes. I was relieved that they were not the co-defendants in the case I was observing but it seemed that they were still discussing their evidence. Did I have a duty to report this?

I quickly responded that I was just watching a trial and waited to pay for my food. I took my ham and cheese panini and nibbled at the burnt edges whilst I waited for the card machine to connect. This was the first time I was encountering my own ethical dilemma.

The men, clearly uninterested in further conversation, turned back to each other. The tall man turned to his friend and mumbled: 'I'm so glad I finished with my evidence. That was torture. You never want to go through this mate. Trust me.'

Crisis averted. This man was no longer giving his evidence.

I didn't know what I would have done if the two discussing evidence had been the co-defendants in the case I was in. I didn't have rights of audience with the Crown Court and so couldn't raise it in court. I wondered whether I would be expected to inform the court usher or even the barristers in the case, or whether in reality I would be expected to mind my own business. I could see other barristers in the queue and started to wonder if they'd been there before, or whether they had just joined. What if one of them had heard the conversation and thought that I was now a part of an illicit discussion?

I finished my lunch and saw my supervisor was calling me. Forever the paranoid pupil, I panicked. I contemplated whether the entire scenario had been set up as a test and wondered how miserably I had failed. I didn't want to have the conversation in the robing room with so many other barristers around, so I went into the ladies' toilets, checked the cubicles were empty and answered the call just in time.

My supervisor was as cheerful as ever and it turned out he was just checking in to see how my morning had gone. I explained what had happened and what I had initially thought. We laughed at my unnecessary panic and discussed that a sensible course of action (had it been the defendant in my case) would have been to raise it with his barrister. He reminded me that if I was ever in an ethical dilemma, I could call someone in chambers for advice or call the Bar Council ethics helpline, which is there specifically to help people with these sorts of ethical dilemmas. And my supervisor reassured me that I was always welcome to call him, or drop him a text if he was in court. After the call my nerves calmed and I realised how lucky I was to have such a supportive and approachable supervisor. All of that stress was entirely unwarranted but I put it down to still being a nervous pupil.

* * *

One of the most controversial ethical questions at the Bar is whether clients should be able to choose the race or gender of their advocates.

A lot of criminal and family work is funded by the Legal

Aid Agency as many clients are unable to afford to pay all or part of their legal fees. For legal aid work, clients will rarely get much say in which barrister is instructed to represent them.

The Bar operates on something called a 'cab-rank system', which dictates that if a barrister has the right level of experience for the case, and is available, then the case will be allocated in a non-discriminatory manner, and they have to take it (albeit with a few exceptions to this rule). At least, this is the concept that operates in theory, it isn't always a reality in practice. Solicitors often choose barristers or chambers that they trust and have relationships with. Many barrister–solicitor professional relationships develop into friendships.

Whilst the cab-rank rule applies to some extent with legal aid work, it applies to a much lesser extent in private work. When barristers are instructed privately the client has a lot more choice in who is instructed. When people are paying fees, they expect to have a choice. However, there are limitations as to how far they can choose who represents them. Whilst a client may ask their solicitor for a barrister matching a particular description, the solicitor has the discretion to filter out any unreasonable or discriminatory requests.

One of the growing areas at the Bar is direct access work. Direct access means that a client is able to cut out the middle person and go directly to a barrister without using a solicitor. Barristers have to be direct access qualified in order to accept instructions from clients themselves and so not all barristers can do it. However, when clients instruct barristers in this way, the cab-rank rule ceases to apply. The client picks the exact barrister he or she wants to represent them. It's practically impossible to stop direct access clients picking barristers on whatever grounds they please as there is no way to monitor what reasons people have.

I have heard clients say that they would prefer a white, male barrister for their trial because judges are mostly white and male, so they might have a better chance with someone who looks similar to them. In 2018, a female Afghan barrister reported that a client sacked her on a case because they wanted a white, male barrister. This attitude is not encouraging for those of us who are from minority groups. These views need to be challenged by solicitors and clerks who have direct dealings with the client.

However, it is not entirely straightforward, as clients may have legitimate reasons for wanting barristers from a particular group, who might be able to better empathise with them or with whom they would feel more comfortable. For example, a female client who has suffered sexual abuse and is applying for a non-molestation order against her male ex-partner might prefer a female barrister. I have had clients who have been left feeling terrified of a lot of men and who are grateful to be represented by another woman, particularly when they are required to talk about their abuse in some detail.

A black client who has little faith in a criminal justice system where they see no one who looks like them might want to instruct a black barrister who they feel may relate better to their experiences.

More cynically, there are also tactical reasons that a client may wish to be represented by a particular barrister. For example, in rape cases male clients sometimes think it is favourable to have female advocates representing them. In a racial discrimination case, a client might request that someone from the appropriate racial group represent them in an attempt to demonstrate that they are not prejudiced.

I can see the Bar moving further in the direction of people choosing the advocate they want to represent them. The internet enables clients – both lay and professional – to look at barristers' profiles and it is becoming easier to ask for a specific barrister.

Providing there is more diversity at the Bar, the cab-rank rule is the fairest way for people to be represented. But at the same time, it is unrealistic to think that the profession won't move towards more choice for clients. It's not dissimilar from other services, such as healthcare. When people pay for their medical treatment, they have greater choice about who treats them; if you receive care from the NHS, you will not be able to choose your doctor. Unlike with the NHS, however, not everyone is entitled to free legal representation. If you earn over a certain threshold, you are expected to pay for your legal representation. The problem is that if people are paying for their representation, they expect to be able to choose their solicitor and their barrister. As there is a move towards more privatisation of legal representation (as legal aid becomes harder to obtain and more cuts are made), there will be more inequality in representation. The richest defendants have the privilege of being able to pay for the most experienced barristers – or those that they consider will be the best asset to them in court.

* * *

Around the same time as Mr Mason was insisting he was not guilty of burglary – at least until after Christmas – I observed my first domestic abuse case. The defendant was disappointed that his advocate was a female barrister and made it clear from the start of the conference that he did not want to be represented by a woman.

The barrister I was shadowing was blunt with him: 'Well, I can leave, if you want? You can try to find someone else at 9.30am when your trial is starting in 30 minutes. It's really up to you.'

The client, Mr King, scowled at her but reluctantly

agreed that she should stay. He was alleged to have punched his ex-girlfriend, Ms Blackburn, repeatedly; thrown hot coffee in her face, leaving her with burn scars, and ripped out chunks of her hair. I read the papers the night before we were appearing in court and looked at the photos of all of the injuries alleged. They were brutal. Her face was black and blue and there were huge bald patches on her scalp. The photos were hard to look at. I was surprised this case had stayed in the Magistrates' Court. But I had to put my feelings to one side and focus on the case at hand. Mr King was saying that he didn't do it and it was his barrister's job to make sure that he was properly represented.

The trial was listed to last only one day and the prison delayed bringing Mr King to court that morning because they were understaffed. This gave the barrister very little time to speak to him ahead of the trial. As it turned out, there wasn't much to talk about. Mr King said he didn't want to discuss the evidence but he agreed that his proof of evidence (a document setting out what the defendant says happened) was correct. According to him, Ms Blackburn was lying about the entire incident.

The document stated that Mr King had been to Ms Blackburn's house that morning but had left around lunchtime to meet his friends. He claimed that he had argued with the complainant (who had been his partner of ten years), because he had ended their relationship and was dating another woman. He alleged that she was distraught and threw household items at him. Sadly, the case was typical of many that come before the magistrates all the time. He said that he stormed out and that when he left the property she was completely fine and had no injuries. He maintained that he didn't commit the offences and did not want to plead guilty to something he hadn't done. The barrister warned him that accusing her of lying would mean that the prosecutor was likely to make an oral application to introduce his previous convictions. He said he didn't care because she was a liar and that she would 'get what was coming to her'. I sat in uncomfortable silence.

The case began fairly smoothly. Ms Blackburn was giving evidence via a video link so that she would not have to be present in the same courtroom as Mr King, but the atmosphere was still tense. Her relatives and friends had decided to come into the courtroom and sat wide-eyed at the back of the room. The prosecutor finished asking Ms Blackburn questions and it was time for the defence barrister to question her. She started with some fairly easy questions to begin with, which Ms Blackburn found it hard to disagree with. She confirmed that she was in a relationship with Mr King for ten years and that she loved him.

'You must have been upset when he told you he was leaving you?'

Ms Blackburn muttered, 'Yes.'

The barrister then began to put Mr King's version of events to Ms Blackburn. The dynamic changed: 'He told you that he had fallen for someone else?'

She was curt in her response: 'Well no, he told me he'd been shagging my friend.'

This was an unexpected turn. Mr King hadn't told us that the woman was Ms Blackburn's friend. The defence barrister remained calm. No one would have known that she was not expecting that answer.

The barrister pushed on with the questioning and asked whether Ms Blackburn was angry, which she reluctantly accepted. The barrister then suggested that Ms Blackburn had lost her temper and started to hit Mr King. She admitted slapping Mr King in temper. The magistrates raised their eyebrows.

We then hit a brick wall. The defence barrister started to suggest that Ms Blackburn was uninjured when Mr King left her property, as per his account. He maintained that she had inflicted these injuries on herself and that she was now blaming him because she was heartbroken. The questions from the defence barrister were thoughtful and precise; she did not prolong the questioning for a second longer than she needed to but it didn't matter. Ms Blackburn broke down. She was crying hysterically and then, to my surprise, she turned on the defence barrister:

'How…can…you? How can you…as a woman…stand

there…and accuse me of lying?' Her voice broke on the last word. She continued sobbing.

The defence barrister paused and allowed her crying to dampen the room. She slowly looked up at the magistrates, who then turned to Ms Blackburn. I could see that her eye make-up had smudged and that she was shaking, even though the live-link screens were a few metres away. The Chair of the magistrates – who sat in the middle of the three magistrates presiding – carefully explained that the barrister was just doing her job and was required to put the defendant's case to her. She noted that it might be uncomfortable and distressing but, in order to have a fair trial, it was essential that the defendant was able to challenge her evidence through his barrister. The views that the defence barrister was putting to her were not the barrister's views and it was irrelevant what, if any, views that barrister had. Her job was to represent her client and best serve his interests and that required challenging her evidence.

Judges, magistrates and juries are not automatically told about a defendant's previous convictions, though the defence and prosecution may agree to reveal them. I observed one case where the client, Mr Kennedy, had a number of previous convictions for assault, which was what he was being charged with. However, Mr Kennedy's record showed that he had always pleaded guilty when he had committed an offence but he was pleading not guilty for the current charge. His previous convictions were brought in to show to the court that although he had a history of offending, he was always honest about committing crimes. This may have bolstered his credibility in his not guilty plea and Mr Kennedy was eventually acquitted.

The printout from the Police National Computer database showed Mr King's previous convictions: a long list of similar offences. Both the prosecutor and the defence barrister were aware of Mr King's record, but there are strict rules about raising convictions at a defendant's trial. Mr King could have chosen to reveal his previous convictions but the prosecutor could not bring them up in court without applying to the court for permission, which is called making a 'bad character application'. 'Bad character' is defined in legislation and includes evidence of misconduct, disposition towards misconduct and reputation for misconduct. Misconduct is defined as 'the commission of an offence' or other 'reprehensible behaviour'. 'Commission of an offence' does not just include previous convictions in the UK and abroad, it includes evidence relating to offences where a person has been charged, even if they were found not guilty. 'Reprehensible behaviour', however, is not defined; it is for the judge to decide whether behaviour is reprehensible. Case law states that 'reprehensible' has an element of culpability or blameworthiness.

There are a number of ways a prosecutor (or a co-defendant) can make an application to introduce a defendant's bad character. For example, it may be important explanatory evidence (meaning it is difficult to understand other evidence in the case without it) or it may be used to correct a false impression that the defendant has created.

In Mr King's case, the prosecution made a bad character application on the basis that his previous convictions for similar offences (against Ms Blackburn and other former partners) were relevant in that they showed that he had a propensity to assault domestic partners. They also submitted to the magistrates that Mr King's previous convictions should be admitted into the case because he had attacked another witness's character: Mr King had argued, in giving his evidence, that Ms Blackburn had lied to be malicious.

Setting aside Mr King's case, the procedure of making a bad character application in the Magistrates' Court can be unfair. The prosecution makes an application to the magistrates who make the decision, but the process feels artificial because, even if I – as the defence barrister – have a compelling argument as to why it would prejudice my client's trial if they consider his or her previous convictions, the fact is that the magistrates have already heard about them. The most the magistrates can now do is to try to ignore them when making their decision. But magistrates are of course human like the rest of us, and can you really completely ignore a piece of information when making a difficult decision?

In the Crown Court it made more sense, as the application is made to the judge, in the absence of the jury. If the judge granted the application, the jury would be told about his previous convictions. If the judge did not grant the application, the jury would not know about them.

In this case, the magistrates did agree that Mr King's previous convictions should be admitted into evidence. He was found guilty and his case was sent to the Crown Court for sentencing as the Chair of the magistrates felt that they did not have sufficient powers to sentence him. Magistrates are only able to sentence defendants to six months per offence, limited to a total of twelve months. He was remanded in custody in the interim given that a custodial sentence was likely.

It wasn't until I got home that evening that I really appreciated how difficult that case had been. It was tough to watch this vulnerable woman break down in a public courtroom about the violence that she suffered. I can't deny that the process of answering all of the barrister's questions must have been traumatic.

But as hard as it was to watch that case, it reminded me that our personal beliefs have no place in our work. A barrister's job is to represent our client in the best way we can by taking their instructions, putting them forward to the court and challenging the contradictory evidence.

I cannot refuse cases on the grounds that I don't align myself with a client. If I could, I would not have represented a large number of my clients, particularly the ones who have openly told me that they don't like black people or that they don't want to be represented by a woman (either not caring or failing to realise that I am both of a black heritage and a woman).

It is vital that we remain independent and the danger with only having clients with views that align with yours is that you begin to lose your impartiality. I quickly learned that our impartiality is central to our job and our job is to do the best for each client, regardless of who they are or what they believe.

4

Breaking the Rules

Mr Smith was what I used to picture when I imagined a barrister; he was a middle-aged white man with grey hair and an expensive-looking suit. He looked like a stereotypical barrister.

I read the case summary again. A barrister, Mr Smith, had sat uncomfortably close to a pupil barrister that he didn't know at an evening drinks event. He kept putting his arm around her, engaging in excessively physical and unwanted contact. He made a number of inappropriate comments, including asking whether the pupil had ever 'taken it from behind'. Whilst Mr Smith might have looked like the stereotype of a barrister, he certainly did not act as a barrister should.

I was getting closer to being 'on my feet' (being allowed to do my own cases) when I was reminded of the consequences of breaking the ethical code that barristers must abide by. I was invited to shadow a barrister acting for the Bar Standards Board (BSB) in a misconduct hearing involving Mr Smith. The case summary reminded me that even in this profession, where we are responsible for upholding the law and expected to act ethically, there would always be those who fell short of that standard.

The BSB is the body that regulates barristers in England and Wales. It sets the standards of conduct for barristers and publishes a code of conduct for us to follow. It handles the most serious complaints made against barristers and punishes them where necessary. This includes reprimands, fines and temporary or permanent suspension from practice.

The first encounter I had with the BSB was sitting the Bar Course Aptitude Test (BCAT). All aspiring barristers must sit the test prior to starting our professional training course, otherwise known as 'Bar school'. If you manage to pass the test, which is slightly oddly graded 'fail', 'pass (marginal)', 'pass', or 'pass (strong)', then the BSB continues to loom over you throughout your year of Bar school. You learn to fear the all-knowing body responsible for ensuring that you maintain the high standards of the profession. Thankfully, most barristers will not have much interaction with the BSB during their careers.

Any barrister facing disciplinary proceedings is entitled to representation and, perhaps unsurprisingly, they will be represented by another barrister. The BSB also appoint a barrister to represent them. Of course, barristers cannot act for the BSB if they know the person in trouble, so any conflicts of interests must be identified.

As usual, I was tasked with taking notes of the proceedings. I generally typed my notes but handwriting felt more appropriate in the otherwise silent room. I had been in over 50 courts in the past few months and yet this small hearing room felt more intimidating than even the grandest of courtrooms. The room was painted a sterile white and was very square. Two parallel rows of two-person desks made the room resemble a classroom. The shorter row of desks was for the tribunal.

Being questioned by your peers is a brutal part of the BSB process. Mr Smith was experienced in his area of law and had been in the profession for over 20 years, which served as a reminder that nobody is above the code of conduct. There was an uncomfortable tension in the room as he was asked how drunk he had been that evening. Mr Smith looked as though he wanted the ground to swallow him as he admitted that he was so drunk he could not recall what had happened. He seemed so alone in this room full of people. I couldn't bear to look up and focused intently on scribing a verbatim record of everything being said.

I heard sniffles and a low moan as Mr Smith was brought to tears. He was trying to speak but I couldn't make out most of what he was saying. I peered up from my notes expecting to see a room of sympathetic expressions but all I saw were blank faces. The process was undoubtedly humiliating and I could hear the quiver in his voice as he was questioned directly. The tribunal asked whether he had put his arms around the young female pupil and had invited her to sit on his lap. They then questioned him on whether he asked how old the pupil was before asking whether she had ever been 'taken from behind'. He could not remember what he had said but didn't dispute it. The members of the panel deciding this case held poker faces as they listened to his responses and jotted down their own notes.

As with any other hearing, we were invited to leave the room for a short period whilst the panel considered their decision. I found a quiet area in which to collect my thoughts. The Bar is not an easy profession to break into and I considered how much this barrister might lose if he was suspended from practice. All of those years of academic study, for a start. Even if you study law at university and go straight into pupillage it takes at least five years from leaving school before you can start practising: three years of a law degree; one year of the BPTC and one year of pupillage. Some barristers, like me, study subjects other than law at university and so are required to do a Graduate Diploma in Law (GDL) for a year – otherwise known as a law conversion course. Also, many barristers don't go straight into pupillage as it's very competitive and often people have to apply more than once. In the interim years many people will often do internships, take on paralegal jobs or some do further masters'-level study. With a minimum of five years of study (and often much more), it seemed like a huge amount to risk. Not to mention the financial loss as there is a huge cost to qualifying as a barrister.

Education and finances aside, being a barrister is a demanding job and there are a lot of late nights and sacrificed evenings and weekends when you start out. I would often find myself at home on a Sunday wondering where my free time had disappeared to, having been in court from Monday to Friday (and sometimes Saturday) and then spending much of the rest of the weekend preparing for the week ahead. The effort put into building a viable practice, especially as a barrister doing a lot of legal aid work (which is not paid as well as private work), cannot be taken for granted. The thought of suddenly losing all that I had worked hard for made me feel anxious.

After the tribunal had spent about half an hour deliberating we were called back. A chill swept through the room but that didn't stop sweat dripping from Mr Smith's forehead. His shirt clung tightly to his body and his collar stood up at an awkward angle. I was surprised that no one had sorted it for him but I guessed that this was not high on anybody's priority list. We nodded respectfully towards the panel and sat down in unison.

The panel had decided that Mr Smith had behaved

in a way that brought the profession into disrepute, particularly as the inappropriate comments and actions had been performed in a public place. Tears trickled from the barrister's eyes into a small puddle on the desk which he wiped with his sleeve. He sniffed and lifted his head to await his punishment.

I had seen this look before, plenty of times, in the courtroom. This man looked remorseful and his actions since the incident suggested that he was sorry for what he had done. He had sent a letter to the pupil's head of chambers expressing his remorse and had voluntarily signed up to a training programme on sexual harassment in the workplace. However, being sorry just wasn't enough.

The tribunal felt that a fine was an appropriate punishment in the circumstances and demanded that Mr Smith satisfy the sum immediately. I noticed a small sigh of relief and a whisper of thanks as he released his neck muscles to again hang his head, this time in both shame and sorrow. He assured the tribunal that he could pay the fine today and began to relax slightly into his chair.

The members of the panel reminded Mr Smith that the details of their finding would be published on the Bar Standards Board's website alongside the punishment that he had received. This meant that anyone searching for his name online could, and probably would, come across this information. I could only imagine the potential impact that this might have on his prospect of getting new clients. He looked as horrified as I was and turned to his barrister with a helpless expression.

The tribunal thanked the barristers who had acted in the case and they stood up to leave. We all stood in unison. The tension in the room made the walk to the door feel far longer than it was. We tried to avoid eye contact with Mr Smith to save him any further embarrassment. The corridor was small and did not make it easy to avoid another person and so I half-smiled uneasily as we inevitably passed each other.

Whilst Mr Smith looked exactly like the archetypal barrister, his behaviour was nothing like I had expected from a barrister. Behaviour like this affects the reputation of the entire profession.

* * *

As the decision about whether I would be offered tenancy in my chambers crept closer, I grew just as nervous about breaking the unofficial rules as I was about breaking the official rules. I was over a third of the way through my 'apprenticeship' but I was still struggling to figure out the social expectations of pupils.

Social etiquette feels just as important as professional attainment during pupillage. This is because the tenancy decision was going to be made by my peers. The tenancy committee would be made up of some permanent members of the chambers and mine and my co-pupil's supervisors. They would recommend us (or not) to the rest of chambers. Then, there would be a vote: the rest of chambers could veto the decision of the tenancy committee.

I got to know many of my colleagues, particularly the more junior tenants, through drinks after court at the pub closest to our chambers. There was an informal rule that pupils were not allowed to pay for anything, which was made clear to us early on. I still tried to buy my own drinks every time because I didn't want my colleagues to think that I expected them to pay, but everyone made a real effort to look after the pupils.

These relaxed drinks were a great way to unwind and offered a real opportunity for me to hear about the junior barristers' work, which I knew I would be starting soon. Sometimes the senior barristers would join us and they would inevitably question me about how I was finding pupillage. I struggled to find the right balance: I wanted to tell them what I had been up to and how interesting all of the work had been but at the same time I was aware that they might not be interested in the intricate details of my diary. I was also always extremely conscious of keeping pace with how much other people were drinking. I didn't want to seem unwilling to fit into the culture of catching up over a drink but equally didn't want people to comment on how much I – as a pupil – was drinking. It felt like I was always second guessing myself.

As a pupil barrister, I was expected to do work for other members of chambers as well as my supervisor. One evening, just before leaving chambers at 6pm, a senior barrister asked me to do some urgent administrative work for him. I didn't know what he meant by 'urgent' and I was so eager to impress him that I decided that it had to be done that night. In hindsight, it would have been sensible to ask for a deadline but I hadn't done any work for him before and I wanted him to think highly of me, particularly as I felt that his opinion was influential in chambers. I started the work and realised that it was going to take much longer that I had anticipated. It was mostly filing and organising papers from his previous cases into various folders, but there were hundreds of pages and I needed to make sure that it was done perfectly.

At 10.30pm I finished and emailed the senior barrister to let him know that I had completed the work and that it would be ready on his desk for the morning. Exhausted, I tiptoed downstairs towards the front door of chambers ready to make my way back home to Essex. I knew I wouldn't be home until midnight and I had to be up again at 6am to head to court. I was already dreading it and hoped I might be able to nap on the train.

But when I got to the front door and tried to open it,

it wouldn't budge. I tried again and then again. It stayed securely shut. It dawned on me that I was the only person left in chambers and clearly nobody had realised that I was still here. I had been locked in! My first instinct was to panic. I had to be at court tomorrow morning and I was worried I'd be locked in chambers overnight. I thought about whether the clerks would be in chambers early enough for me to get out and head to court on time. More importantly, we didn't have any beds in chambers. All I had was the clothes I was wearing.

I called my parents. They found the situation hilarious. Their recommendation was to nap on the sofa in the waiting room and 'surprise' the clerks in the morning. I couldn't think of a better way to ensure that I did not get offered tenancy.

I messaged two of the junior tenants who provided me with the senior clerk's number but there was no answer from his phone. Feeling desperate, I called my supervisor.

'Alex, are you stuck in chambers? Oh my goodness. You couldn't make this up.' Like my parents, he found my predicament humorous.

I clumsily explained that I didn't know how I would make it to court tomorrow as he was trying to hold back the laughter. I was convinced that this was the end of my dream of becoming a barrister. My supervisor, once he'd stopped chuckling, reassured me that he had a key for the front door. I was relieved but embarrassed that it had come to this. He set off from home to travel all the way into central London in the middle of the night to let me out of chambers. I was mortified. When he arrived, I sheepishly thanked him and headed home to recover as many hours of sleep as I could.

This wasn't the only late night during pupillage; there were many late nights and very early mornings. Sometimes this would be because there were networking events going on until late in the evening and other times I was just trying to finish the work that I had been asked to do. My supervisors would always make it clear that I should tell them if I was struggling with the amount of work but I was cautious not to create the impression that I couldn't handle the high pressure of the job.

I thought back to the conversation I had with my cousin about whether or not I would fit in to this environment and I was determined to prove that I could. My solution was to make time for everything I was asked to do, even if it meant working into the early hours of the morning when I had court the next day. This would add to my general feeling of exhaustion and I became even more reliant on my morning coffee.

I wondered how long it would take me to learn all of the unspoken rules. For example, a number of people had nicknames, or seemed always to be called by their surnames, but I wasn't sure whether I (as a pupil) was invited to call them by these names. Playing it safe, I stuck to only addressing them by their first names, even if it meant I was the only one doing so.

At an Inn event, I was scolded by a fellow pupil at another chambers for admitting that I would shake hands with an opponent at the end of the case if it was appropriate. She warned me that 'barristers never shake hands', which seemed ridiculous. I asked around and learned that this custom stemmed from barristers not wanting to give their clients the impression that they were working with the opponent. Whilst I understood the reasoning, it seemed nonsensical given that working productively with an opponent often seemed to get clients the best results. The adversarial nature of the Bar is excellent for disputed issues but often there is much agreement between parties and it seemed pointless to create a false impression of hostility.

I worked on some child arrangement order cases, where a parent applies to the court for their children to live with them or spend time with them, usually after the parents separate. I'd observed that it was in both parties' best interests to have representatives who could work well together. In such circumstances, handshakes with the other legal team at the end of the case seemed appropriate.

The cumulative effect of following both the formal and the informal rules of the Bar added pressure. I felt out of my depth and wondered how so many other pupil barristers seem to know them before doing the job. I wanted to demonstrate confidence but it was difficult when I felt overwhelmed by all of the subtle, unwritten rules that I was expected to abide by but didn't always know.

However, as I was struggling to get to grips with the subtle social and professional codes of chambers, I began to appreciate that many people who come into contact with the justice system hadn't learned about or didn't understand the laws that governed them.

Mrs Bush was appearing in the Magistrates' Court, accused of assaulting someone she used to call a friend, Ms Green. The incident had taken place outside Mrs Bush's house. They'd had a verbal argument about their children. It seemed that Ms Green's child had claimed that Mrs Bush's daughter had been bullying her and Ms Green had come to Mrs Bush's home to speak to her about it. The argument took place on the doorstep and escalated into a shouting match. At one point, Ms Green had turned to walk away and Mrs Bush had grabbed her arm. Ms Green pushed her away, which caused Mrs Bush to fall back onto her front door. Ms Green then left the property.

I was shadowing the barrister who was representing Mrs Bush in court today. She accepted grabbing Ms Green, which had not resulted in any physical injury. However, under the law this amounted to an 'assault by battery'. An assault by battery describes when a defendant intentionally or recklessly inflicts unlawful force on another person. There was no doubt that Mrs Bush had intentionally grabbed her former friend and that this force was unlawful because the friend had not given her permission, implied or express, to do so.

Mrs Bush was distraught that she had been caught up in criminal proceedings because of this incident. The words 'assault by battery' sounded so serious to her and she cried the entire time during the pre-court conference before her hearing.

I found myself sympathising with Mrs Bush as I listened to her talk to her barrister. Although the police and the courts expect everyone to abide by the law, most people are never formally taught what is a criminal offence and what isn't. A lot of our education about the law comes from our parents or from rules at school, but it isn't always clear to people how serious the consequences can be. Not knowing that your actions amount to a criminal offence is also not a defence for most crimes and so people can be – and are often – punished for things that they did not realise were against the law. Mrs Bush had no previous convictions and had never been in any trouble with the police before.

The reason that this had ended up in court was because Mrs Bush had answered 'no comment' in her police interview. She said that she had panicked in the police station and that her solicitor had told her to do so. The police then escalated the matter to court. If she had admitted to grabbing her friend during the police interview, the matter could have been dealt with using a police caution.

In court, Mrs Bush pleaded guilty. The magistrates were sympathetic to the circumstances and only imposed a conditional discharge, which meant that if she did not re-offend over the next six months she would face no punishment for this offence. She was ordered to pay £85 in costs and a £20 victim surcharge.[1] She continued to cry as she was being sentenced.

Outside of court, Ms Bush asked about the impact that this conviction would have on her employment; she was worried about how it might affect her job and whether she would have to tell her employer. She was particularly concerned that this would show up if she ever had to have a Disclosure and Barring Service (DBS) check – a criminal record check carried out by employers.

Her barrister explained that the offence would be recorded on the Police National Computer (PNC) database indefinitely. Until the order finished (in six months' time) it would also be 'unspent', which meant that

---

[1] The victim surcharge is a penalty applied to everyone convicted of an offence in order to provide compensation for victims of crime. The money does not go directly to the victim (as with compensation) but is distributed to support victims and witnesses.

it would need to be disclosed to employers, insurers and for some financial checks. After six months, it would be 'spent' and would not be disclosed on a basic DBS check. However, she was warned that it could always be brought up in any future criminal proceedings, even when the six-month period was over.

Mrs Bush was very distressed and I could see her beginning to cry again. I rushed to offer her some tissues. She said that she was likely to lose her job as she regularly transported children to and from school. A criminal conviction can have such a vast impact on a person's livelihood.

Whilst some defendants are ignorant of the law, others are willing to risk a criminal conviction because they feel they have no other choice. These are the hardest cases.

Mr Taylor was arrested for possession of an offensive weapon and today was his first appearance. His barrister gave me a summary of the case as we were heading down to the cells to meet him. He was 19 years old and had been stopped and searched and was found to be carrying a knife. This was his second knife possession offence and he was facing a mandatory six-month custodial sentence.

In the cells, his barrister told Mr Taylor that he was facing prison. He looked petrified. He barely looked 15, let alone 19, and he had spent the previous night in police custody. Mr Taylor reluctantly explained that he didn't know what the court and police expected him to do in his circumstances. His voice quivered and I could see his hands shaking as he spoke. Although he was not in a gang, his brother was part of a well-known gang and on the day of the offence, he had to travel through an area where rival gang members operated. The last time he had been in that area was two years ago, when he was just 17. On that day he had been attacked by a group of six boys and had ended up in intensive care. He lifted his shirt and showed us the extensive scarring across his chest.

Carrying a knife for your own protection rarely amounts to a defence in law. The defence of having a 'good reason' for carrying the knife only applies if a person is in fear of an 'imminent attack'. It is a matter for the jury as to how imminent, how soon, how likely and how serious this attack will be.

Mr Taylor wanted to plead guilty. His mother attended court and waited patiently to speak to his barrister while we were in the cells. When we returned to the waiting area, she told us about his learning difficulties and the post-traumatic stress disorder (PTSD) that he had suffered as a result of the attack two years prior. She provided copies of some medical appointment letters from his doctor and his counsellor to show the court.

In court, the prosecutor argued that, according to sentencing guidelines, this offence fell into the highest category of culpability because a knife is a bladed article (as opposed to an offensive weapon that is not bladed, for example a knuckle duster). Yet she conceded that it could be deemed to be in the lowest category for harm given that he hadn't carried it in a school or a place where vulnerable people were likely to be, and no one had been caused serious alarm or distress because he had not brandished the knife.

In response, the defence barrister explained to the judge what had happened to Mr Taylor just two years earlier, in the same area. The barrister spoke with such compassion and I listened carefully. She reminded the judge that since Mr Taylor had pleaded guilty at the first opportunity, he should be given credit (a discount on his sentence). The defence barrister acknowledged the mandatory minimum of six months imprisonment for this offence but asked the court to consider suspending any custodial sentence (so providing Mr Taylor did not commit further offences in a set period, he would not have to serve the prescribed custodial sentence). She suggested that, as a punitive measure, the court could consider imposing an electronically tagged curfew on Mr Taylor, especially given that he had been stopped with the knife late in the evening.

The judge listened carefully before determining Mr Taylor's sentence.

He asked Mr Taylor to stand and sentenced him to a 21-week custodial sentence, which he suspended for two years. He added: 'Mr Taylor, you must also undertake a Rehabilitation Activity Requirement for 30 days, focusing on weapon awareness. You will be under an electronically monitored curfew from 8pm until 6am for 3 months.'

Mr Taylor was relieved. He had to pay prosecution costs and a victim surcharge but was so pleased that he was avoiding a custodial sentence.

'Thank you, Judge,' he whispered from the dock.

I turned and smiled at him and he grinned back. I could see that his eyes were red where he had clearly been crying. I couldn't imagine how nerve-wracking it must be, at such a young age, to be sitting in a dock waiting for a judge to tell you whether or not you will be going home or sent to prison.

I learned an important lesson from Mr Taylor's case that day. Laws are not always broken for selfish or greedy reasons. Mr Taylor had been desperate and scared. He had been brutally attacked and he was, understandably, terrified for his safety. He knew that carrying a knife was wrong, as he had a previous conviction for the same offence, but he was so scared that he thought that the risk was worth taking.

Mr Taylor's case affected me, having lost Ayo to knife violence, and it was devastating to see that a young person felt that the only solution was to arm himself with a knife for protection. Not only was he breaking the law but he was bringing another knife onto the streets that might be used to attack someone else or be used against him. But I had never been in his position, so I couldn't say what I would do in his situation.

Observing these different cases taught me so much about why people break rules or commit crimes. Clearly it wasn't as simple as everyone knowing the law and people choosing not to obey it. Some people only realise that they have broken the law once they are caught up in criminal proceedings. Other people know the law but feel as though the risks involved in breaking it are worth taking. My job isn't to judge people in either of these circumstances; I represent defendants once they are already in front of the court and try to ensure the best possible outcome for them.

5

Where Are the Women?

People often imagine that courtrooms are held in the grip of tense silence, the judge's careful pauses making room for the echo of his or her last words. Before I started my training, I imagined that everyone would sit there tight-lipped, scared to cough or sneeze. During my first few times in court, I was nervous of breathing too heavily or moving too suddenly, worried that I would interrupt the solemnity of the courtroom.

In reality, there is often quite a bit of hustle and bustle in the courtroom. Hushed whispers are exchanged between barristers and ushers debating whose case will be on next. You can hear the muffled voice of the clerk calling another courtroom or calling probation services to make enquiries about the current case. Nobody is worried about coughing and I have often had to pause for ten seconds when making my closing speeches to allow someone to have their coughing fit. There's also often shouting: sometimes from the judge, sometimes from a witness and sometimes from a defendant. In fact, the only people who I have never heard shout (in the courtroom) are the barristers. There are mumbles and grumbles and usually at least one stomach rumble. There is sometimes snoring and, although the snorer is usually a member of the jury, I've seen police officers, solicitors and even a judge fall asleep in court.

As a trainee barrister in the first six months of pupillage, encouraged to take a note of everything that is happening in the courtroom, you notice all of the sounds in the room, from the low conversations to the witness's nervous taps on the witness box. You debate whether to include *everything* that is said in your notes, verbatim, or whether to leave out the mutters under people's breaths that they may not have intended others to hear. You witness the speedy and sharp translation of everything that is being said in English into the language of the defendant, and back the other way. Interpreters are blessings in disguise because in the time they are translating, you have a few extra seconds to type.

One afternoon I found myself assisting a senior prosecution barrister in a multi-handed (i.e. more than one defendant) fraud trial. The defendants were builders and were accused of fraudulently overbilling clients for work done by altering invoices from the contractors that worked for them. There was a lot of paperwork in the case as there were a number of original invoices and many alleged doctored invoices. We were in a small courtroom and not all the barristers could fit in the front row, especially given all of the paperwork, so the co-defendant's barrister joined me in the row behind.

The barrister I was shadowing was impressive. He was eloquent and persuasive and commanded the jury's attention in a way that I had never seen before. They lapped up his every word and I could see the jury members nodding along as he spoke. Tapping away, I entered the prosecutor's words:

'The defendant's evidence is circumscribed...'

The senior defence barrister next to me chuckled and leant closer than was necessary to me. His greasy forehead shone even under the dim light of the courtroom. He was close enough that I could see the faint wrinkles under his eyes and I could smell the musty fragrance of his morning coffee on his breath.

His voice lowered and he whispered: 'I'm not *circumcised*.' The wordplay sat uncomfortably in the small space of air between us. 'I'm not *circumcised*, because I'm Catholic.' He chuckled again at his own joke and sat upright and continued to write in his blue lined notebook.

I shuffled along the wooden bench to distance myself from him. I looked up and around to see if any of the other barristers had heard but they were fixated on their laptop screens. The comment had disturbed me; I felt very uncomfortable. I'd heard the horror stories of sexual harassment at the Bar and, naively, I thought that it wouldn't happen to me.

This emphasised to me the practical importance of having better representation of women at the Bar, particularly at the senior end. Women often feel more comfortable talking to other women about sexual harassment or sexism at work. Even if women are not willing to report sexual harassment to senior women, the mere presence of more senior women may reduce the prevalence of sexual harassment. Had there been more women in the courtroom that day, this barrister might have thought twice about making his 'joke'. I wondered whether he would be as comfortable saying something like this in the presence of a number of equally senior or more senior women. I highly doubted it.

There was a huge imbalance in the power dynamic that morning: I was a pupil barrister and he was a senior barrister. I knew that he had intended the comment as a joke but, frankly, I had no interest in whether or not his penis was circumcised and talking about that with a woman at least 20 years younger, in a courtroom, felt entirely inappropriate. I was in the training year to qualify in the job he was already senior in and he knew this.

I didn't know who to report the incident to or whether I even should. The other barristers in the case were male. The judge was male. My supervisor was male. I worried that I might be seen as an overly sensitive female who couldn't take a joke.

In reality, pupils are unlikely to approach the Bar Standards Board, either. Pupillage is a year-long interview, in the course of which your peers decide whether you should be kept on at the end of the year. The Bar is a 'small' profession, in the sense that people tend to know a large number of the people in their practice area. I felt that I couldn't report this incident to the barrister's chambers because there was a good chance one of his colleagues would know someone in my chambers. All it would take was for one person to deem me to be a troublemaker. In this job, reputation is everything and as a pupil the 'pupillage paranoia' tells you that reporting inappropriate behaviour might result in that reputation being damaged.

The problem of sexual harassment at the Bar, and the difficulties some people might face in reporting it, hasn't been completely ignored. The Bar Council– the organisation that represents barristers and acts as a voice for the profession – worked with a technology company to create an artificial intelligence bot, called 'Talk to Spot', that enables barristers to record sexual harassment and other bullying anonymously. The Bar Standards Board will only be able to investigate a report if the barrister chooses to manually submit their report. However, while the app is brilliant in theory, in reality it's very difficult to use it to identify and punish anyone guilty of harassment.

In order for any tribunal to be satisfied that something has happened and for the person responsible to be appropriately punished, it will often prove necessary for the complainant to be identified so that the alleged perpetrator has the opportunity to defend themselves. Many people are likely to still feel the same fear of jeopardising their career by making an allegation, even with this app.

In February 2019, the BSB released a report on diversity at the Bar.[1] The report revealed that women and men were entering the profession as pupil barristers in roughly equal proportions – in fact, there are slightly more females than males: 54.8 per cent and 45.2 per cent respectively. However, women are underrepresented at the senior end of the profession. Queen's Counsels (QCs) are the most senior members of the Bar, recognised for their experience and excellence. The statistics show that 38 per cent of barristers overall are female, but at QC level only 16.2 per cent are female. The effect of this can be felt throughout the profession, even at the most junior end.

The drop off seems to coincide with the age at which a lot of women choose to start a family. Anecdotally, a lot of women in my age group have said that they are considering not starting a family because they are worried about how

---

[1] https://www.barstandardsboard.org.uk/uploads/assets/912f7278-48fc-46df-893503eb729598b8/Diversity-at-the-Bar-2019.pdf

it will interfere with their career. The Bar, as it currently stands, has a long way to go until it is family friendly.

Most barristers are self-employed (approximately 80 per cent of the profession[2]), which means that, as with many other self-employed professions, barristers are only entitled to statutory maternity or paternity pay, which is minimal. Many women return to court shortly after having their children because they cannot afford to remain off work without pay.

One lunchtime, in the robing room, I overheard a middle-aged male barrister complaining to a similarly aged female barrister about having to pay his chambers' rent (the fee you pay to your chambers to work there) during his period of parental leave. He was only off work for two months but he said he was outraged that he had to continue to pay during this time. His experience had made him realise how difficult it must be for women, particularly those who have no choice but to take more time off. The female barrister chuckled at his outrage and jested that that was why she had chosen not to have children. I wondered whether that was a joke or a serious comment. Either way, I realised that continuing to pay rent during parental leave was a factor of self-employed life that disproportionately affects women at the Bar.

---

[2] https://www.barcouncil.org.uk/media/177469/bar_barometer_nov_2012_web_upload_higher_res.pdf

Whilst unpaid parental leave and paying 'rent' may not be exclusive to barristers, the amount of time that it takes for self-employed barristers to be paid exacerbates the issue. A barrister friend of mine recently squealed with delight that she'd finally been paid for a case that she'd completed 18 months ago! The knock-on effect of this delay is that when a barrister takes time off for parental leave the financial burden might not hit them straight away.

Speaking to a colleague in chambers, I realised that during the first few months of parental leave barristers continue to receive an income because of delayed payments for cases they took on before parental leave, and in fact the difficult period often begins when they return to work. Until speaking to her I hadn't fully appreciated this. She explained that instead of returning to work and receiving a stable salary, she was a new parent who was working hard but actually had little money because she had not been invoicing in the months that she was off. Of course, this problem hits other self-employed people who have issues with aged debt but it's particularly problematic in a profession that already struggles to retain women.

The concept of paid parental leave has been explored by some chambers already. A collective chambers pot could pay parents for up to an agreed number of months while they take parental leave. In a conversation with junior tenants from a mix of chambers at the pub one evening, I asked what they thought about paid parental leave. There was a mix of views and one female junior barrister said, quite bluntly: 'I don't see why I should have to pay for someone else to have children.'

I was a bit taken aback by this comment. I felt as though it completely missed the point of supporting our colleagues. As members of the Bar, we would be sacrificing a small amount of our income to improve retention of women in our profession. By making it more affordable to have children, we would hopefully help to encourage women to return to the Bar as a financially viable career.

Even as a barrister without children, I've seen how difficult it is to manage personal commitments. In one case, I had been at court since 9am with a barrister who was making a bail application for her client. She had told the court usher that she needed to be away by lunchtime for a medical appointment. The usher was helpful and reassured us that she had passed the message to the judge, but warned that there were a lot of cases in the courtroom that day.

It was approaching 1pm when the case was finally called. The client had been arrested for burglary and the judge was faced with the possibility of imposing a custodial sentence. The judge said that she would make the decision about whether to grant him bail after lunch as it was approaching 1pm. The barrister I was shadowing explained that she had to leave for a medical appointment. The judge refused to let her leave. I was surprised that medical appointments were treated so flippantly and I realised how difficult it would be for parents to leave court for childcare arrangements. But as a self-employed person, booking an entire day off to go to the doctor for example makes attending any appointment very expensive. I can only imagine how this is exacerbated when, as a parent, you have appointments for you and your children.

I noticed other factors that adversely affect women, who tend to be primary carers, too. Many of the women in my chambers who have children find it more difficult to make the networking events. There is a lot of networking at the Bar, mostly with solicitors at drinks and lectures, and the vast majority of it is in the evening. I rarely make it home in time to eat dinner with my family.

I'd already travelled to more places in England than in my entire life prior to starting my pupillage. One of the things I loved most was that no day was ever the same, but this unpredictability negatively affects parents who have to adhere to some kind of school or childcare routine.

The irregularity of our diaries also makes part-time work almost impossible. Whilst I could, in theory, only work on particular days, as a criminal or family practitioner I would lose a lot of good quality work. In criminal law cases, the court will ultimately decide when a trial is scheduled and, whilst they may try to accommodate a barrister's working preferences, it's impossible to do that if the trial is expected to take a certain number of days. For instance, if I only work three days a week, but I have a client with an estimated two-week trial, I have to either increase my working week or hand the case to someone else. Even if the hearings are short, there may be difficulties scheduling cases on specific days to suit my working arrangements.

The court's priority is to deal with cases efficiently and often this will preclude a client being represented by the same barrister at every hearing, even where barristers work full time. In an important family case I observed when I was first a pupil, where the judge had to decide whether a baby was going to be taken into local authority care, the judge had to set a date for the next hearing that some of the barristers in the case could not attend. The local authority, the parents and the grandparents were each represented by barristers who had conflicting diaries and the result was that one of them had to find cover. Of course, it is in the best interests of the client to have continuity of representation but sometimes it is inevitable that different barristers will be instructed because of diary clashes.

Of course, many of the issues affecting women at the Bar also affect women more widely, including female clients.

The case that stands out to me the most is one in which a client was nine months pregnant and was still asked to attend the Magistrates' Court for her trial. The baby was due any day and, at one point, while giving her evidence, the mother-to-be had to leave the courtroom and go to the bathroom with her partner as she thought that she was going into labour.

Her barrister made an application for the trial to be adjourned but the magistrates refused on the basis that they did not want to create delays, especially when the court would otherwise sit empty. Given there was no other reason to proceed, it would have been fairer for the court to allow the adjournment and wait until the baby was born. But the magistrates seemed unwilling to consider that it was inappropriate for her to be giving evidence in her condition, and once she returned from the bathroom they continued with the case and eventually convicted her of a public order offence for shouting at a neighbour and making him feel alarmed. She was ordered to pay a fine.

Though the offence was not particularly serious, because she had a trial (which uses court time and resources) she was also ordered to pay substantial costs. As a mother-to-be she was worried about the financial position that the fine and costs would put her in but the court made it clear that this money needed to be paid as soon as possible. In the end it was decided that it would be deducted from her benefits, which she was very concerned about given that she was about to give birth, but she knew she had no other way to pay.

Often, female clients do not have alternative childcare provisions for their children and so are forced to bring young children along to court with them. Whilst most courts will not usually allow children in the courtroom, many judges make an exception when a mother attends with a small child because no relatives or friends are available to sit with the child outside the courtroom. If the judge refuses permission, as I have seen happen, the barrister will usually go into court and represent the client without them being there. This can be difficult because the judge will often have questions that can only be answered by the mother, who is left waiting outside court. It is impractical for a barrister to be repeatedly leaving the courtroom to check things with their client. Courts can be very stressful environments and, whilst every effort is made to deal with cases quickly, there can sometimes be lengthy waits, which are even harder for women with young children.

Many female clients say how happy they are to see another woman representing them in court. In the family courts, where women are often asked invasive questions about their personal life, this can be especially important. Perhaps unsurprisingly, family law is one of the few areas of law where women are better represented. Resolution, an organisation representing family lawyers, legal executives, barristers, financial experts and family therapists, reported that 27 per cent of its members were male and 73 per cent female.[3]

I have been in family law cases where everyone in the courtroom is a woman, except for my client's ex-partner, which is something I have never experienced in the criminal courts. They are male dominated in a way that the family courts are not. A possible reason for this is that family law is seen as a 'female' area of law, because of the sensitivity of the issues that are dealt with and how many 'soft skills' are needed in dealing with clients.

However, if women are going to be treated equally and properly represented at the Bar, it is important that women are represented in all areas of law, not just family law.

* * *

'My advice to other pregnant women at the Bar? Get a partner if you don't have one already (or make sure your mother or some other family member lives next door).'[4]

A barrister, perhaps half-jokingly, gave this advice to female barristers in a newspaper article. She added: 'I've

---

[3] https://resolution.org.uk/wp-content/uploads/2020/01/resolution-diversity-data-report.pdf

[4] https://www.theguardian.com/law/2011/apr/28/barristers-solicitors

never met another single mother at the Bar (I have met those who have subsequently split with their partners but still share the finances). There is undoubtedly a reason for that.'

The question lingers of what can be done to help improve retention of women at the Bar. It's clear from comparing how many women enter the profession to how many reach a senior position that this is a problem, though the data available is insufficient to determine exactly when women are most likely to leave the Bar. But ultimately, the Bar will always be at a disadvantage if we fail to retain women. Not only is it important for our clients to see balanced representation in the courts, but judges and barristers who have their own families bring a wealth of experience to the profession. In family law, where the courts try to help rebuild and support families, it seems incredibly ironic that many barristers have to choose between having a family or pursuing a career at the Bar.

Women are initially welcomed to the Bar and the statistics show that. We need to make sure that women are also encouraged to stay and that there are measures in place so talented women don't have to make a choice between having a family or continuing in their career. As a junior barrister, I have been grateful for the mentors I have had but I would like to see more role models and support networks to guide young female barristers in this traditionally male-dominated profession. If a client only sees men at all stages of the legal process, they might, understandably, question the equity of the system determining some of the most important issues in their life. The court system is where we look for justice and fairness.

As a woman, I have at times felt uncomfortable, particularly when people have made inappropriate jokes or comments whilst I am at work. It worries me that this behaviour continues and I think a large part of it is because of the macho culture in the courtroom. The legal world has been male dominated for a long time. It was only recently that we celebrated 100 years since women first entered the profession. For things to change, women need to remain in the profession and reach the top ranks.

6

You Don't Look Like a Barrister

Nothing can prepare you for taking on your first case on your own. There is a huge transition from shadowing your supervisor to being 'on your feet'[1] in front of a court, representing and advising your own client.

After just six months I was now trusted to represent clients, without any assistance or supervision. My supervisor had signed the relevant forms for the Bar Standards Board, confirming that I had observed the relevant items on the 'pupillage checklist'[2] and I was being sent out to court on my own. I was nervous; my clients would expect me to have the answers and my advice might be taken as gospel. But I was also excited – I was finally allowed to speak on behalf of my client in court.

---

[1] We use the term 'on your feet' to describe when we begin representing clients. Presumably it describes us literally standing 'on our feet' in court addressing the judge or magistrates.

[2] The 'pupillage checklist' is a document provided by the Bar Standards Board that must be signed off by a pupillage supervisor at the end of the six-month shadowing period and again at the end of the second six-month period where pupils take on their own cases. For the first six months, the checklist includes items such as 'preparing jury bundles', 'attending a Crown Court trial' and 'drafting a defence statement'. https://www.barstandardsboard.org.uk/training-qualification/becoming-a-barrister/pupillage-component/pupillage-forms.html

My first ever client, Mr Greggs, had been caught speeding five times on different roads over a period of a few months. On another occasion he had hit a fence and failed to provide his details to the police when sent a letter about it. I hoped that his solicitor had been realistic with him about the outcome of this case. He was almost certainly going to be disqualified from driving.

I had read Mr Greggs's papers more than ten times over the weekend. I didn't quite have all of the documents that I needed, but having shadowed other barristers for the last few months I knew that I was lucky to have received at least some of them, as often they don't arrive in time. I was grateful to have had the time to prepare. I had planned every word I was going to say to my client and had my advice written out perfectly.

I arrived at court at 8.30am, half an hour before the doors would be opened. It was early April and it was still cold outside but I couldn't risk being even one minute late. I had my wheeled suitcase with me but it felt quite empty because I didn't need my wig and gown. Barristers don't wear their wigs and gowns in the Magistrates' Court for criminal cases (they are only worn in the Crown Court and other higher courts). I had recently discovered that wearing a black dress saved on ironing a white shirt every day, so I was dressed head-to-toe in black, with a suit jacket on over my smart work dress.

One of the missing documents was a copy of my client's driving record. I had ambitiously hoped for a copy of his driving licence too. It would have been a useful document given that I didn't know what my client looked like. At 9am the doors were opened and the public began to arrive. I confidently called out: 'Mr Greggs? Is anyone here called Mr Greggs?'

No one answered.

I repeated my call every ten minutes. It was creeping towards 10am, the start time of our hearing. I knew there were many other cases listed in the same courtroom and I didn't want to be stuck here all day. I called Mr Greggs's solicitor's office to see if they had any idea as to his whereabouts, or could find out, quickly, and was waiting on hold when a young man dressed in a navy tracksuit, burst through the door. He was clutching his phone in one hand and a bunch of keys, including a car key, in the other.

I introduced myself. He smiled as he greeted me: 'What, you're my barrister, yeah?'

I nodded and matched his grin.

'Oh wow. You don't look like my other barristers, that's for sure.' He winked and slumped on to the chair next to me.

I thanked him for the compliment and clumsily moved the conversation on. I always felt awkward when a client commented on my physical appearance. Having shadowed both male and female barristers I realised that this happens far more frequently to women than to men. On one of my 'mini pupillages' (a work experience placement, in other words), a defence barrister approached me in the robing room to tell me that her client had asked her to pass his mobile number on to me. Given that he had just been sentenced to eight years in prison, she joked that she had told him that I was unlikely to have much use for it. I knew she was only conveying a message but it made me feel uncomfortable in a professional environment.

I led Mr Greggs into a conference room and began to advise him of the likely outcome of today's hearing. My meticulously prepared script was quickly set aside as I realised that he knew more about driving offences than I had anticipated. He had previous driving convictions and knew that, in any event, he was facing a driving disqualification today.

'Alex, look, I have a baby on the way. My missus is ready to burst and she don't drive.' Mr Greggs looked at me like a child, his eyes wide open.

I made a note of what he was telling me.

'I don't want to have to send them out on a bus, you know what I mean? I can't afford taxis.'

Mr Greggs wanted me to argue that he would face 'exceptional hardship' if a disqualification was imposed and asked me to make that argument to the court. If the court is satisfied that a driving disqualification will cause a person exceptional hardship, they can choose not to disqualify a person, despite them accumulating 12 points or more on their licence (which is the threshold for mandatory disqualification). Whilst I understood the point that he was making – using a car was more convenient with a new-born child – I pointed out that many young families have to use public transport. I also warned him that the court might expect him to sell his car.

'Nah, they can't force me to do that. No way.' His voice was getting louder and he began to get more agitated.

Reassuring him that I was just advising him on what the court may expect, we moved on to his financial situation. He explained that he worked for himself and didn't have any savings. Handing him a 'means form' (a form on which defendants are trusted to declare their income, outgoings and savings), I explained that this was how the court would consider his financial circumstances. He filled it out and handed it back to me. I warned him that if a disqualification was imposed, he would not be able to drive his car from today's hearing. He shrugged, unbothered.

As we entered the courtroom, nerves started to bubble inside me. The three magistrates determining this case came into the courtroom and the usher formally called on our case. The prosecutor set out the facts of the offences and applied for the defendant to pay costs.

The magistrates nodded and turned to me: 'Yes, Miss Wilson, what would you like to say?'

It was my turn. I felt adrenalin running through me. I stood up slowly and started to speak; the confidence in my voice caught me by surprise. I didn't need to rely on my notes as I articulated the mitigating factors about my client. There was actually little to say about the offending behaviour. Mr Greggs had admitted that he was speeding whilst testing out his new car. I informed the court about his financial circumstances and handed up his means form. I explained that he had a new baby on the way and conveyed how important it was for him to be able to use his car.

My client then took an oath and stood in the witness box. I asked him a series of questions to elicit the information that he had told me – chiefly how difficult and impractical public transport would be with a new-born baby. The prosecutor asked some follow-up questions but barely challenged my client's account. Things were going surprisingly well.

It was the Chair of the magistrates' turn to ask her questions.

'Mr Greggs, you've said you were testing out the speed of your new car?'

He smiled sheepishly: 'Yes, I am sorry. It was stupid but I've learnt now.'

The magistrate paused. 'Do you own your car?'

He nodded and mumbled 'yes'.

'Well, you could sell your "new car" and that would help with any public transport costs and might help with any fine we impose today.'

Mr Greggs looked as horrified as when I had suggested it. He explained that he had no intention of selling the car as he would never be able to afford another one, but the three magistrates looked unimpressed.

They retired to consider their decision. I waited in court hoping that, even if they didn't accept that a disqualification would cause exceptional hardship, they might be sympathetic to what I had said about his financial circumstances.

Twenty minutes passed and the usher knocked on the door and invited us all to stand while the magistrates came back into the courtroom. I looked up at the huge crest hanging over them as they settled into their seats. I tried to read their expressions but they kept poker faces and tidied the papers in front of them. The Chair began to read their decision.

'So, Mr Greggs, we have listened to what has been said regarding the hardship but we are not satisfied that there is exceptional hardship. It is not accepted that you and your partner cannot use public transport, however unattractive that may be to you.'

I looked at Mr Greggs who had his head in his hands.

They continued: 'We have looked at all of your offences and are imposing a 12-month disqualification. It is going to be a "totting up" disqualification.[3] You will pay a band C fine of £120 for failure to provide driver details. We are not giving any further fines for the five speeding offences. You will pay prosecution costs of £135 and a victim surcharge, which everyone has to pay, of £30.'

The Magistrates explained what a 12-month disqualification meant whilst Mr Greggs nodded along. He agreed to pay the costs at £40 a month.

We left court and Mr Greggs reached into his pockets and retrieved his phone. I asked if he had any questions but he didn't; he said he was just glad we didn't have to wait around all day. I was relieved that the costs were relatively low. We made small talk about how cold it was outside as I headed towards the exit and he followed closely behind.

As we departed, he called out, 'Do you want a lift to the station, Miss?'

I turned around to see that he had his car keys in his hands. He smiled at me and waited for my response, jingling the keys impatiently.

Panicked, I reminded him that he shouldn't be

---

[3] A 'totting up' disqualification is a driving disqualification for a minimum of six-months, which is imposed if a person has received 12 penalty points or more on their licence within a three-year period.

driving. He was disqualified for 12 months. He chuckled and smoothed his hair with his hand. He didn't take this seriously. Incredulous, I turned my back and marched towards the station, keeping my eyes firmly down on the pavement.

* * *

Within the first few weeks of taking on my own cases, I realised how fleeting my involvement is in people's lives. I arrive at court, usually having never met my client before, and expect them to trust me with some of the most important decisions in their lives.

Unsurprisingly, many of my clients have been taken aback to see someone so young acting for them. I am often asked 'how long have you been in the job?' and 'how old are you?' Once I start speaking about the case and my client realises that I am thoroughly prepared and know what I am talking about, I can see that they begin to feel more reassured, but it always feels unnerving justifying my presence.

I often notice how surprised my clients are to see a woman appear to represent them. I tend to use 'Alexandra' professionally and I have lost count of the times I've been mistakenly referred to as 'Alexander'. If I introduce myself on the phone to a solicitor as 'Alex', they pass on a message to the client that 'Alex' will meet them and there tends to be an assumption from many lay clients that 'Alex' is a man.

One client, Eve, made it very clear that I stood out. She was young, just 19 years old, and was charged with criminal damage for breaking her bedroom door and window in her supported housing.[4] One of the other young people in the accommodation had called her a racial slur and she was alleged to have lost her temper. She had pleaded not guilty at her first appearance in court but the evidence was strong. Two support workers had seen her cause the damage and were attending court as witnesses. She had also apologised immediately after the incident, in front of the support workers and the police officers who attended the property.

I took her into a conference room to discuss the case. She explained what had happened that day. I understood how upset she felt when her housemate had repeatedly tormented her with racial jokes. It was clear that she had had enough. She knew it was wrong to punch the door and smash the window. She accepted committing the offence and said that she would plead guilty.

Just as I stood up to leave the conference room, she called me back. 'Alex, you know, you don't look like a barrister.' She had a kind smile on her face and I knew she

---

[4] Supported housing is an umbrella term that describes housing schemes that support people to live independently. For example, this can include people who have mental illnesses, learning disabilities, have grown up in care and people who are homeless.

meant this as a compliment.

I returned the smile and reassured her that barristers come in all shapes and sizes.

She laughed and sat back in her chair before commenting, 'It's nice to have a black lawyer. You get it. I tried to explain this to the other lawyer I spoke to and she didn't get why I was so upset. That's why I didn't trust her when she told me to plead guilty; she wasn't even listening to what I said.'

Those words stuck. She trusted me.

We went into court and she entered her guilty plea. The court adjourned until the afternoon so that a pre-sentence report could be completed (this is done by the probation services to help the court decide on the most appropriate sentence). As we headed out of the courtroom, I heard her belly rumble and she nervously giggled. I told her that she was free to get some lunch but that she should meet me back in the waiting area in 45 minutes' time. She nodded and I departed to retrieve my belongings from the advocates' robing room.

I returned to the main hallway a few minutes later and saw her sitting in the same place, hands in her lap and no lunch in sight. I asked whether she had any money to get lunch. She shook her head and I felt my face reddening for having been so insensitive. I invited her to follow me and we went to a nearby café where I bought her some food. It dawned on me that my job sometimes requires me to be so much more than just a lawyer.

The judge decided to give Eve a conditional discharge. They explained that, providing she did not reoffend over the next 12 months, she would face no further punishment. The case was over as quickly as it had started. She thanked me for my help and said that she was relieved that the case was finished. I knew that I might never see this young woman again but I hoped that my momentary involvement in her life might have helped her.

* * *

As I progressed into my second month of taking on my own cases, my diary got busier. I had cases every day and often I wouldn't find out where I was going until I arrived at chambers at 9am.

On one such morning, at around five to nine, I buzzed into my chambers, coffee in hand and stuffing the remainder of a breakfast muffin into my mouth. Before the front door even closed behind me, I was given a name, a court and the clerk's assurance that if any papers arrived, they would be sent on to me by email. I turned around and scurried back to the station, hoping to make it to a court on the other side of London before 10am – the time the case was listed for. A big gulp of my scorching hot coffee and I was off, excited and ready to meet my client who I hoped (and prayed) would turn up.

I refreshed my inbox on the train and saw that an email had flown in. It was a 'first appearance' for a man named Mr Fuller, which would be fairly straightforward and required a lot less preparation compared to a trial. What a relief.

Everyone who is charged with a criminal offence and has to attend a criminal court will have a first appearance at a Magistrates' Court. It is exactly what it says on the tin – the first time you appear in front of the court for the offence you are charged with. Offences are divided into three categories. 'Summary only' offences, such as low-level driving offences, can only be tried in a Magistrates' Court. 'Either-way' offences, such as most thefts, can be tried in the Magistrates' Court unless the magistrates or judge feel that it is too serious and send the case to the Crown Court. The defendant can also elect a Crown Court trial. The main difference is that in the Crown Court a jury decides whether you are guilty instead of a magistrate or district judge.

Juries are usually made up of 12 members of the public; magistrates are also lay people but they see criminal cases every day in their work, as do district judges. Some defendants elect a jury trial because they feel that a jury is more likely to be fair, as they can be more objective in assessing the facts of the specific case in front of them rather than being influenced by the many other cases they have seen.

Indictable-only offences are the most serious and include offences such as murder and rape. These cases can only be heard in the Crown Court. When dealing with a first appearance for an indictable-only offence, the hearing is very straightforward as the case is sent to the Crown Court and, in most of these cases, the only thing for the magistrates to consider is whether to grant the defendant bail.

If it's an offence that the magistrates are permitted to deal with, a defendant will be asked how they want to plead: guilty or not guilty. If they plead guilty, the court will either adjourn for a probation services officer to speak to the defendant and complete a pre-sentence report (so that the court can make a more informed decision about sentence) or the defendant will be sentenced there and then.

If a defendant pleads not guilty, the court will prepare for trial. For example, they will decide which witnesses will be attending. Witnesses only need to attend if one of the parties (the prosecution or the defence) needs to cross-examine them about something that they have said in their witness statement. If what is said in a witness statement is agreed by both parties, the witness will not need to attend court to give live evidence.

Mr Fuller had been charged with theft and assault of a police officer, and the case looked as though it would be staying in the Magistrates' Court. These were the sorts of offences I had been observing in the Magistrates' Court when I had shadowed junior tenants in my chambers. Most of my work in the first few months of taking on my own cases would be in the Magistrates' Court dealing with this sort of thing.

At a first appearance, I advise my client on what the law is in relation to the alleged offence(s), the evidence that has been produced by the prosecution and give them information about the possible sentence they may face if they are convicted of any or all of the offences. We also talk about any possible defences and any witnesses or other evidence that might be able to support their case.

When I arrive at court for a first appearance, I never know whether it is going to take a few hours or the entire day. One of the reasons that it can take a long time is because there might be a large number of cases on the court list being heard before my case – any of which could overrun. Or, the conference with my client might take a long time because there are so many issues to deal with. This is particularly likely when a client has been charged with multiple offences.

First appearances are shockingly underpaid, regardless of the barrister's seniority. The Legal Aid Agency only pays £50 (before tax), which means that if I am at court all day (which has often been the case) I am paid just £5 an hour and that doesn't include any preparation time or time spent writing a note to the solicitor after the case.

For these hearings there is relatively little time to prepare the case because it is rare to get the papers earlier than the day before the hearing. On many occasions, like this day, I receive the papers on the morning of the hearing, or even once I arrive at court.

I arrived at court at 9.45am. I placed my bags in the airport-style security scanner, wishing I was in fact on the way to some exotic location for an all-inclusive holiday. I emptied my pockets and the security team searched my bag. One member of staff fumbled at the bottom of my bag and pulled out what he thought might be a suspicious item, only to then realise that he was parading my tampon to the rest of the court attendees in the queue. His face reddened and he quickly ushered me through the metal detector before his colleague scanned me with a handheld device. I received the all clear and proceeded to dump my stuff in the advocates' robing room before rushing to court to apologise to the usher.

The courtroom was only just being unlocked as I arrived at the door and the usher greeted me with a keen smile and asked if I was ready for Mr Fuller's case. Embarrassed, I promptly replied 'no' and asked whether my client had signed in with her yet, which he had not. I headed into the main waiting area and loudly called out for him. I was met with a crowd of shaking heads. An elderly woman asked me whether I had called for her and I assured her that I didn't. She sighed and turned away. Relieved, I sat down and waited.

I began to read through the documents provided: the summary of the offence, the witness statements and the exhibits. Mr Fuller had been accused of stealing meat from a supermarket and assaulting an officer once he was arrested. The meat was found in his bag and the police summary claimed that the CCTV evidence showed a man looking remarkably similar to Mr Fuller.

I looked at the CCTV footage: the man had long, dark hair pulled back into a limp ponytail and a considerable amount of facial hair. His stomach protruded and the absence of a belt became increasingly obvious as he heaved up his trousers every few seconds. The culprit was dressed in the same distinctive clothing that my client was allegedly arrested in: a bright multi-coloured vest, loose jeans and luminous green flip flops, despite it being a pretty cold December day. The man on CCTV was seen entering the supermarket, taking the meat and hiding it under his vest. The irony of him putting chicken fillets in his top made me laugh.

The police officer had also produced pictures of his

reddened arm that Mr Fuller was alleged to have caused in slapping the officer away at some point following the incident. Again, the incident was recorded; the police officer had proudly exhibited stills taken by his police body camera. The man I saw in the pictures was clearly the same man that I had just watched conceal meat in the CCTV footage. I closed the papers and reminded myself of the sentencing guidelines for each of the offences.

It was now ten o'clock and so I called out again for Mr Fuller. My voice echoed around the waiting hall and mixed with the sounds of a baby crying and some fuzzy music blasting from a man's headphones. I reached for my phone and called the solicitor. The receptionist informed me that the solicitor was not at his desk and asked me to try again within the next hour.

Another 15 minutes passed and the usher confirmed that my case was being called on next. I called the solicitor again. The solicitor answered this time and I explained that Mr Fuller had not yet attended court and asked whether they had received anything from him to suggest he may be late or not attending. He hadn't but he tried to find a contact number for me.

I knew the solicitor was busy and I felt like I was wasting his time asking him to chase our missing client but I had no means of contacting Mr Fuller directly. In most cases, the solicitor is the link between the client and the barrister.

This is a blessing in many ways (for instance, it means we don't have clients calling our phones in the early hours of the morning when they are arrested) but it can be frustrating and inefficient when we need to get through to our client.

It was bad news. The solicitor realised that all previous correspondence had been via email and that they didn't have a telephone number on file for him. (It's not unheard of for a client not to have their own mobile phone. Some communicate with their solicitors via a library computer. But of course, this means we have no way of getting hold of them instantly if we need to.) He asked me to wait at court until 11am as he was sure the client would attend, as he had responded to an email reminding him of his court date. In Mr Fuller's notes, I had read that he had previous convictions for 'failure to surrender' (not turning up to previous court hearings) and worried that the solicitor was being overly optimistic.

I nervously walked into court, bowing to the judge as a sign of respect as I entered. The judge asked me for an explanation as to where Mr Fuller was and I had nothing to offer. I explained that I had been in contact with my instructing solicitor but he did not have a contact number on file. The court clerk looked at her computer and noted that the court had a number recorded for Mr Fuller. The judge put the hearing back for 15 minutes and asked that

I try to get hold of him myself. I noted down the digits carefully and assured the judge that I would try my best to reach him. I left the courtroom as quickly as I had entered.

The phone didn't even ring, it beeped and then a flat tone sounded. I tried again and this time it went straight to a generic answerphone. I tried a third time, just for luck, and again it reached the mobile's answerphone. It seemed hopeless.

The 15 minutes flew by and I was called back into court. I reported this to the judge who considered whether a warrant for his arrest needed to be issued. I tried to reassure the court that I didn't think that was necessary and the judge gave me until lunchtime to ensure that Mr Fuller arrived. She warned me that if he did not, a warrant for his arrest would be issued and his bail would be withdrawn. This meant that he would be kept in custody.

I retired to a broken chair outside of the courtroom so that I could keep a careful eye out for anyone who might be my client. The problem was that almost any male entering the building could have been my client. Whilst I had the CCTV footage and the police officer's body-worn-video stills, this wouldn't have been the first case where a client hadn't looked like the images provided by the police. Sometimes my client clearly was not the person who had committed the offence and other times the quality of the images was so poor that nobody could be made out from them. I didn't know what Mr Fuller looked like or anything about him. In fact, I considered that someone could walk into court and claim that they were him and I would know no different.

It's alarming how trusting the court system is. Defendants do not have to provide physical ID when they appear in court and no photographs or fingerprints are taken, which means that there is no way of verifying that the defendant, or any witnesses for that matter, are who they profess to be. I am surprised that there aren't greater concerns about this given that someone could potentially use a false identity and give evidence as someone else. Of course, if someone were to be given an immediate custodial sentence the person pretending to be them would be in a difficult situation, which I suppose is a deterrent in at least some cases.

At 12.30pm the solicitor called to say that he had received an email to say that Mr Fuller's estimated time of arrival was 1.30pm, as he had mistakenly thought it was an afternoon hearing. I sighed and opened my laptop to try to make a dent in some of the work my supervisor had set me. One of the most difficult things about pupillage is trying to manage your own work in court as well as ensuring that you adequately complete written work for other members of chambers. What with long days at court, completing work for other barristers and further training or networking in the evenings, it can feel like pupillage has become your whole life.

After what felt like forever, Mr Fuller turned up. I had waited around for him all morning and I was keen to get this conference started.

'Sorry I'm late,' he began. 'I don't have anywhere to live at the moment, I'm homeless.'

I looked up at the man standing before me. It was devastating to see yet another client struggling with poverty. The Ministry of Justice's research reports that 15 per cent of newly sentenced prisoners say they are homeless before going into custody (compared with just 3.5 per cent of the general population) and 37 per cent reported that they would need help finding a place to live when they were released.[5]

Mr Fuller continued, 'I thought court was this morning but whenever I come to court, I have to wait around. I thought I might as well go to the shelter and try to shower and even get some food first.'

I could hear the defeat in his voice and it reminded me why I should never be too quick to make assumptions about a client's personal circumstances when they arrive

---

[5] Ministry of Justice, Accommodation, Homelessness and Reoffending of Prisoners: Results from the Surveying Prisoner Crime Reduction (SPCR) Survey https://assets.publishing.service.gov.uk/government/uploads/system/uploads/attachment_data/file/278806/homelessness-reoffending-prisoners.pdf

late for court. Many of my clients live in very difficult circumstances and even getting to court is burdensome. I told him not to worry too much but warned him that the court may expect him to explain why he failed to appear at court on time given he was told that he must attend for 10am. To avoid dwelling on his lateness any further, I invited him into a conference room to discuss his case.

The conference rooms at that court are small and better described as conference cupboards. The chairs and the table were screwed to the floor and it didn't take much of an imagination to figure out why the court had decided to implement this. This court building must have seen a lot of violence though because I had only ever seen this before in a prison. Standing outside the conference rooms, we could hear every conversation inside, which completely undermined the point of having private conference rooms. However, it was slightly better than not having a separate room to use at all, which is the case in some court buildings.

So we crammed into one of the conference cupboards and my client began to tell his story of what happened, starting with how he'd noticed that meat had increased in price over the past two years. I stopped him. Whilst I was genuinely interested in his backstory, the court would be starting again at 2pm and we really did need to get to the crux of things. He looked startled by my interruption but now was not the time for niceties. The most important thing today was that I represent my client to the best of my ability and I could only do that if we talked about the issues in the case.

I advised him on the damning evidence against him and showed him the CCTV footage. He tried to maintain a straight face while he looked at each picture but gave in to laughter when he saw how clearly you could see his face.

'Could we tell the court that the CCTV has been fiddled with? Like, could we say it's fake?' He could not hide his smirk.

My response was blunt: 'Well, is that you?'

'Of course! But we might as well try.'

He looked up at my straight face and his smirk disappeared.

'OK. Yeah, that is a dumb idea,' he mumbled.

Addressing his question, I briefly explained the difficulties with suggesting that the video was doctored. He paused me mid-explanation.

'You know, I haven't ever seen a barrister like you before.'

I relaxed my stern face and asked whether he meant that as a compliment. He laughed nervously and confirmed that he had. He said that I sounded 'so normal'.

'You from Essex?' he asked.

I nodded. He proudly told me that he could tell from my accent and that he was glad that I was the person representing him. I laughed with him. I was pleased he felt that way. Mr Fuller relaxed and the tension dissolved between us. He felt at ease and it transformed the conference.

Mr Fuller decided that he was going to plead guilty to stealing the meat but not guilty to assaulting the police officer. He maintained that it had been a reflex reaction to the officer leaning too close to him and that he had not intended to injure him. I went to speak to the prosecutor who was willing to withdraw the assault charge providing Mr Fuller pleaded guilty to the theft charge.

I highlighted to the court that he had no money and that, whilst it was not excusable to steal, he was not stealing for profit; he was stealing to eat. I explained that he was currently homeless and asked that they consider not requiring him to pay any prosecution costs, given his financial situation.

The judge recognised that neither a fine nor costs would be appropriate in these circumstances. Exceptionally, they gave Mr Fuller a conditional discharge: there would be no punishment providing he did not reoffend in the next six months. He was relieved and tried to kiss my hand to express his gratitude.

'Normality' is different for everyone. If clients can see diversity in the barristers that represent them, they are more likely to trust us. Mr Fuller became more comfortable and began to speak more freely when he guessed that I was from Essex. It was a sense of familiarity that got him on side and broke down the perceived barriers between us.

People caught up in the criminal justice system might have more faith in it if the Bar is more diverse. They will see barristers who look, and sound like them. It can be reassuring to walk into a room and not stand out because of your skin colour, gender, accent or socio-economic background.

Whilst I might be different from the traditional idea of a barrister, in lots of situations this can make me more relatable and may mean that I am able to foster trust much more easily. Ultimately, a barrister's job is to represent the public and the public is not just made up of middle-class white people, which has been the composition of the majority of the Bar for far too long. Britain is growing in diversity and the Bar needs to grow with it. My clients are from a wide range of socio-economic backgrounds; they have different accents from different parts of the country, as well as different nationalities and ethnicities. We need the Bar to reflect this so that the public feel confident that we are diverse enough as a body to be able to relate to and understand their circumstances – otherwise how can they trust that the system is fair?

7

More Than Meets the Eye

I headed down into the Magistrates' Court's cells to introduce myself to my client – a stubbly, dark-haired man with a strong Scottish accent who was in court for his first appearance. The offence was assault: he was alleged to have thrown a glass at another man in a pub.

I entered one of the small cells and noticed that there were no tables or chairs, just a single bench. So I sat down next to my client, Mr Brown, pulled out my laptop and loaded up his case papers. Mr Brown strongly denied the offence and claimed he had accidentally knocked the glass and it had flown towards the complainant and had 'bounced up' onto his chin, leaving a bruise. His thick Scottish accent was soothing and I found myself listening to more of the backstory than was strictly necessary.

I glanced at the clock and realised that the court was ready to begin. I gathered up the papers and sprinted out of the cells, telling my client that I would see him in the courtroom. The usher smiled with relief that my case was ready to go. Courtrooms wouldn't run efficiently without ushers. Ushers are expected to make sure that the cases flow one after another and that no court time is wasted. They are responsible for making sure that witnesses are in the right place at the right time and they ensure that defendants take their oaths properly. They are often given long case lists to manage and if cases aren't ready when the court is ready to hear them, it can cause a backlog. I thanked the usher for her patience as we entered court. Mr Brown was brought up from the cells into the dock. He introduced himself to the court, confirming his name and date of birth. He was asked for his address as the court did not have one on the court file. The address he gave was in Scotland, which was unsurprising, given his accent. He confirmed that he did not have an English address and the court clerk entered this information into her computer.

The judge dealt with the case swiftly and efficiently. Mr Brown pleaded not guilty and we handed up the case management forms confirming that we wanted all three of the witnesses to attend court to be cross-examined at the trial. The dates were set for the trial and I tapped away at my keyboard, trying to ensure that I recorded all of the fundamental details.

I made a successful bail application and Mr Brown was asked to report to the police station closest to his house twice a week leading up to the trial. The judge asked whether Mr Brown had a mobile number that he could be contacted on and he responded that he didn't own a phone but he promised that he would turn up next time. Thankfully, there was nothing on his court record to suggest that he hadn't turned up in the past. In response, the judge warned him that the court would not tolerate lateness.

Mr Brown thanked the judge profusely, referring to her as 'Your Majesty' multiple times, rather than 'Madam'.[1] The judge didn't blink at being called 'Your Majesty' and concluded the case. I lowered my head in the direction of the judge out of respect and then turned and left the courtroom.

As I returned to the cells, Mr Brown was collecting his personal belongings and getting ready to leave court. I reminded him of the dates, particularly the next date he was due to attend. He pulled a mobile phone out of one of the plastic bags of his possessions and made a note. It took me several seconds to realise that this was the same device he had just denied possessing.

Mr Brown shoved his phone into his pocket and signed the relevant forms for the cell staff. He thanked me for my time and said he was grateful to have been granted bail. I

---

[1] A district judge or magistrate is addressed as 'Sir' or 'Madam'. Some solicitors also refer to the magistrates collectively as 'Your Worships'. A circuit judge is called 'Your Honour'.

stopped him at the end of that sentence and asked him what he had just said. Mr Brown repeated it with a perplexed look on his face. The words made sense but the accent didn't match. In just 20 minutes, he had gone from having a thick Scottish accent to having a south London accent. As though my thoughts were printed on my forehead, he chuckled to himself.

'Oh yeah, sorry about that, Miss. I'll see you around, yeah. Cheers again.'

I was speechless. I left the cells and went upstairs to collect my own belongings from the robing room.

Aside from being utterly confused, part of me was impressed that my client had maintained an entirely different accent throughout a conference with me and then a court hearing. I wanted to go back down to the cells and ask why he had changed his accent. Was it merely to mask his identity? Did he think that another accent might make him more attractive to the court?

For the rest of the day I worried about that case. I called Mr Brown's solicitor after the case to fill her in on what just happened.

'Ah, I haven't met Mr Brown. I've taken over this case from a colleague.' The solicitor had no more of an idea of where he was from than I did. She placed me on hold whilst she reviewed his file. She picked the call back up and spoke sharply: 'Unfortunately we don't seem to have any address for him on our system,' she sounded worried, 'who is this man?'

I had no idea, and realised that I would probably never find out. I knew I wouldn't be representing Mr Brown at his trial as I already had another case in my diary for the date his trial was set for. I questioned whether anything he had told me had been true and I wondered how his case would pan out.

My job revolves around using my voice and so it's hardly surprising that I pondered the 'dual-accent man' on my journey home. I called a friend and told her about my strange day and she couldn't stop laughing at the fact that I hadn't detected that he was putting on an accent. I promised her that it was more realistic than she imagined. I could see the funny side but it was also strange and troubling.

I reflected on whether, in some smaller way, I change my accent when I'm in court. In just eight months of pupillage I learnt how important it is to be able to adapt your voice and manner for inside and outside the courtroom. I have grown to love my Essex accent and hope I never lose it but my 'court voice' is a bit like my mum's 'phone voice' – everything is properly enunciated and I speak slowly and clearly to ensure that there is no room for misinterpretation. I don't think there's anything wrong with having a 'court voice'; it's a formal setting and speaking clearly is essential.

I grew up on the border of east London and Essex. Sadly, the Essex accent is often ridiculed. It is an accent that is rarely associated with intelligence or professionalism, despite there being a host of talented people who have grown up in Essex.

Unsurprisingly, I first became conscious of my accent when I moved away from home. At home, my family and friends sounded similar and I took for granted that no one assessed my intelligence or capability on the way I spoke. I had successfully competed in debating competitions as a teenager. Nobody had ever commented on my accent and I guess I lived in a bit of a bubble because of that.

This changed drastically at university. In my first few weeks at Oxford, I was described by one girl as 'the one who doesn't sound like she should be at Oxford'. When I asked what she meant, she mimicked my accent and clarified that she didn't think I sounded intelligent. I was devastated. Was she right? I knew that people like me weren't attending Oxford en masse, but I hadn't expected to be singled out so early on.

The girl who made the comment was in the 'popular crowd' in college. The same girl continued to mock my Essex accent and never hesitated to make me feel out of place. At one of the formal dinners in college, she told me to slow down when I was eating my soup because it 'wasn't going to run off anywhere'. I felt like a child being scolded.

I found myself trying to fit in with these people, trying to alter my accent. My every move was highly scrutinised. When I spoke, other students would often reply 'shut up!' in an exaggerated Essex accent followed by fits of laughter.

Although my accent isolated me at university, I started to embrace it in my professional life. Many of my clients tell me that they appreciate how 'normal' I sound.

* * *

Mr Brown's change in accent had left me questioning who he was, but he wasn't the only client to surprise me. I was instructed to represent a client in a trial where he was alleged to have failed to provide a blood sample to the police when stopped for suspected drug driving.

At 5pm the evening before, I received the documents outlining the prosecution case – this generally includes a case summary, a police interview summary, witness statements and my client's criminal record. Although I'd received the papers at 5pm, I'd been asked to stay for a chambers networking lecture and by the time I got home it was almost 11pm and I still had so much work to do. Now I had this case to prepare for. The tiredness was really kicking in. During pupillage you really are working on a magic roundabout where you wake up, work, go to court, go to an event, work and sometimes sleep. If you're like me, you'll find time to squeeze some fast food into your day but many barristers seem to skip meals altogether.

The next morning, I stood shivering outside the Magistrates' Court as the minutes rolled past 9am. Other court attendees began to knock on the glass doors, bellowing that the court was supposed to open at nine o'clock and, although the banging was perhaps unnecessary, I was grateful that I wasn't the only one frustrated that the doors were still closed.

A sheepish-looking security officer eventually came to the front door and twisted the lock, immediately after which everyone tried to squeeze themselves into the first partition of the revolving door at once. I waited patiently, clenching and unclenching my fists to keep the blood supply flowing in my hands, before joining the clamour at the door, looking forward to feeling some sensation in my fingers again.

Finally, I was inside and the security checks began. The man in front of me wanted to take his branded lemonade drink bottle into the courtroom, even though it had a dark brown liquid inside (clearly not lemonade). He refused to taste it and kept claiming that it was 'against his human rights' to force him to drink when he wasn't thirsty. I could see his frustration growing but the security officers remained calm, as if oblivious to his raised voice and flailing arms. The man was clearly anxious and I suspected that whatever was in the bottle might be his attempt to numb that anxiety but there was no way he was going to be let in without proving to the officers that it wasn't either alcohol or a harmful substance. There have been cases of people bringing acid into court buildings and the courts have to be vigilant to prevent these things happening again.

Everyone has to abide by the court's security rules. The fairly obvious one is that you can't take knives or sharp objects into court, which has sometimes proved problematic when people have had their lunch forks or spoons taken away. There are also strict rules about liquids. You cannot bring perfume, deodorant or liquid make up into the court building or else it will be confiscated. Unlike in airports, there isn't an exception for liquids under 100ml.

The only liquids that make it past security and into the court building are drinkable liquids and, to prove that they are drinkable, the court has a 'taste it or leave it' policy. This makes it awkward when you have popped out to get a coffee for your supervisor. You have to politely warn your colleague that you've already sipped their drink. We share a lot at the criminal and family bar.

I was ushered around the commotion made by the man with the strange brown liquid. The contents of my bag were emptied out for the remaining queue to see. I was asked to sample my water and I complied without hesitation, though I regretted it instantly, as the water had been sitting in my bag for at least a week and tasted both warm and stale. The inner zip pocket of my purse was checked for small blades and my bottle of foundation was taken out of my make-up bag and I was asked to sign a slip for it, given a receipt and told to collect it at the end of the day. My gym clothes were held up to the light, as though I might conceal something in my sports bra. I kept my gym clothes in my work bag, ever hopeful that I might finally get some time to go to the gym.

Finally, I passed the checks and was allowed to step through the metal scanner. The alarm sounded, as the universe had clearly decided that I hadn't been delayed enough at the entrance of this court, and a friendly security officer scanned my body with a metal detector wand. Nothing seemed to set the wand off and I twirled around for the officer to scan me from behind. As I scraped up my coins from the plastic tray one of the security officers joked that I needed to be careful to not spend it all at once. I smirked, knowing that I would be spending every penny I had on a very strong coffee that morning!

I hurried to the advocate's room and dumped my bags in a corner. Someone had left their half-eaten sandwich on the table at least a few days ago and there was blue fluffy mould creeping around the edges of what remained. It was obvious that this advocate's room was not visited by any court cleaner and I was cautious not to touch anything that I didn't have to. I retrieved my laptop from my bag and the charger, just in case it hadn't actually charged last night. Heading out, I pulled down my dress, straightened my collar and went in search of my client.

The usher told me that my client, Mr Noah, hadn't yet signed in. Though she also told me that often clients don't ever sign in and so she wasn't particularly surprised. I smiled politely and began to wish there were sleep pods in court for barristers to have a quick nap whilst waiting for their clients.

Mr Noah's defence for failing to provide a blood sample when stopped for suspected drug driving was that he had a needle phobia and was too scared to consent to the blood test. The main issue I could see was that the solicitor had not been able to instruct a medical expert to prove this phobia was genuine because, despite being advised to the contrary, Mr Noah was adamant that he didn't need one.

I opened up my electronic copy of *Blackstone's*, the criminal law practitioner's handbook. I reminded myself of what would amount to a 'reasonable excuse': an excuse the court would accept as a genuine reason as to why he did not agree to give a blood sample when the police had stopped him for his driving. A real fear of needles would be a reasonable excuse, but the question for today was whether the needle phobia was genuine. I was worried that Mr Noah wouldn't be able to show that he really did suffer from this phobia without a report from a professional.

I looked up at the clock and nearly an hour had passed with no sign of Mr Noah. This was becoming a surprisingly common occurrence. I rang the solicitor's office. No one answered the phone. I sent a quick email to the solicitor and decided to scan the building to see if Mr Noah might be waiting in the wrong waiting area on the wrong floor.

I started with the top floor and peered through all of the glass windows of the conference rooms, though it was unlikely that he was lurking there, as a barrister or solicitor would have asked him to wait outside so that they could use the room for a conference with their client. Half of the courtrooms seemed to be locked and closed, which made my search slightly easier. I avoided the men's bathroom and proceeded to search the ground floor. I even checked the cells just in case he had been arrested overnight and nobody had realised, which had happened to a previous client.

Once I'd searched the whole building, I decided that there was very little I could do at this point. I had learned over the past months that there are a multitude of reasons as to why clients might not turn up. Mr Noah was expected at 9.30am. It was almost 11am and no one had heard from him. I couldn't wait around all day for someone who might never turn up.

I popped into court to find the usher and tried to mouth to her that my client still hadn't appeared. Unfortunately, the message didn't translate as intended. It seemed that she thought that I was confirming that my case was ready and called it on with a friendly smile. I smiled back appreciatively. It was my fault for trying to mouth a message to someone on the other side of a courtroom when so much else was going on at the same time.

I stood up to address the judge and apologised for not, in fact, being ready to proceed with my case. I told them that Mr Noah hadn't made it to court yet but that I was in the middle of making enquiries as to his whereabouts. Unfortunately, I did not have any signed instructions from him and therefore could not act on his behalf in his absence.

The judge was dissatisfied with my answer and lectured me on the importance of arriving on time to court. I bit my tongue, remembering the cold wait outside the front door at 9am, and smiled politely, reassuring the judge that I would emphasise this to Mr Noah when he arrived.

As a barrister, you often bear the brunt of other people's frustrations. Your client will tell you how angry he or she is at all of the decisions the judge makes. The judge will complain to you about something another barrister or a solicitor has done or, more often, your client's actions. Whilst it is sometimes helpful to clarify the situation, often you act as a pin cushion and take the hits to ensure the smooth running of the case.

I nodded courteously at the judge and turned to leave

the courtroom, tripping over a laptop lead as I left. I heard a whispered apology but kept my head low to avoid any further embarrassment. As I rushed into the corridor, I let out a huge sigh. Everything was OK, nothing serious had happened, but I still hated being told off in court. It made me feel like a naughty child.

I traipsed back to the advocates' robing room and sunk into an uncomfortable chair. Flipping open my laptop, I began to get on with some of the work for my supervisor. I hardly had the energy but the piece of work was due that evening and I was no longer hopeful that I would be out of court at a reasonable time. This particular court was known to keep going until the list was finished, even if that meant that barristers had to stay in court until almost 7pm. I had a feeling that today might be one of those days.

Around 45 minutes later, whilst I was desperately trying to get in touch with the solicitor's office, my name was called out on the court speaker system: 'Can Ms Wilson report to reception immediately?'

Hearing my name startled me as I had become so used to blocking out the incessant speaker system calls throughout the day. They can be very distracting when you are in a conference with a client and you have to pause whilst the speaker calls for 'Mr Smith to come to court four' (for the seventh time). They are like staff announcements in a supermarket but more irritating.

They are either dangerously loud so that they terrify the living daylight out of you and you have to stop everything that you are doing immediately or they are a muffled buzz of sound and you have to decipher whether the announcement was anything to do with you. This time I was relieved that the speaker system was deafeningly loud as it sounded as though Mr Noah might have turned up, and there could be a chance of starting this case before lunchtime. I gathered my stuff as fast as possible and began to make my way to reception.

'Can Ms Wilson *please* report to reception *immediately*?' The booming voice was stern and bounced off each wall of the small advocates' room. I felt the other barristers and solicitors turn their heads to wonder why I hadn't left yet.

As I approached reception, I could see a heavily tattooed man with a beer can in his hand shouting at the security officers. One of the security officers appeared to be seconds away from restraining him. The commotion was attracting quite a lot of attention. I just wanted to find my client and get on with it.

I looked around but I couldn't see anyone sitting down and nobody seemed to be waiting by reception. I called out for Mr Noah and there was no response. I glared at the man causing a scene as his shouts were overpowering my calls. I tried again, louder this time, to call out my client's name.

The seemingly drunk man paused his shouting and

turned towards me. I had internally muted his voice and I could see him flailing his arms around and spilling his drink down his sleeve. I was not in the mood for a confrontation with a drunk person and was happy to leave security to deal with him whilst I narrowed down where Mr Noah was.

I tuned in to the sound: 'Are you my lawyer? Are you Ms Wilson?' He turned to shout at the female security guard. 'These IDIOTS won't let me in.'

Ah, so he was Mr Noah. I walked over to him and picked up on a strong smell of marijuana. Turning up drunk and high to court when you had refused to provide a blood sample for suspected *drug* driving. You could not make this up.

Mr Noah's arms were covered in tattoos! A needle phobia? Really? His tattooed sleeve was seriously impressive. The colour work made his arm look alive; the tattoo artist clearly had talent. However, these tattoos wouldn't do much to help his defence today.

He downed the last bit of liquid in his beer can and stumbled though the security scanner. As he passed through, he heaved and let out a huge belch which he blew in my direction. Today was not going to be the most glamorous day of my career at the Bar.

The court security team would not let him into court in his current state and I had to explain to him that I would have to ask that his case be adjourned to another day. The court reluctantly agreed, given that it was unlikely that there would even be enough time to hear the case that day in any event. I only hoped that on the next occasion he would turn up sober and on time.

These cases certainly aren't the ones that pupil barristers dream about. When you study the academic side of criminal law, you learn about all kinds of legal-sounding defences: self-defence, involuntary intoxication (where someone has been 'spiked') and duress (where a person acts in fear of serious injury or death). But then, once you move on to pupillage, you learn that there are so many defences and not all of them are as exciting as the ones taught in criminal law classes. Some of them are technical defences, where a person might not be found guilty because of a police officer's procedural failing. Or, as with Mr Noah's claim of needle phobia, a person might allege that they had a genuine reason for acting in the way they did, or not acting, and that may amount to a defence.

You dream about defending the innocent person who has been framed for the gangland murder that he didn't do. In reality, I had accepted that such trials wouldn't be in my diary for a while as the early years are all about building up experience. It's almost certainly a good thing as I don't think anyone charged with murder would feel confident having a fresh-out-of-law-school barrister representing them.

The Bar is slightly unusual in that, unlike many other professions, there aren't a huge number of titles showing each person's level of seniority. There aren't associates, managers, vice presidents, CEOs, etc. There are just pupils, junior barristers and Queen's Counsel (QC). Essentially, once you graduate from pupillage and become a tenant, you are considered a junior barrister. This only changes if you are appointed as a QC.

A junior barrister is often not very junior. Informally, people often distinguish between 'junior juniors' and 'senior juniors'. There is no real rule as to what amounts to a 'senior junior' but, from my perspective, it is probably a barrister who has been in practice for approximately ten years or more. In essence, the majority of the profession are juniors and, since only a small number of barristers are chosen to become QCs (they only make up 10 per cent of the profession), the majority of barristers will remain as junior barristers throughout their career at the Bar.

As a pupil barrister I didn't spend much time with Queen's Counsels, who are the most senior barristers. A QC is also known as a 'silk' because they wear special silk gowns to highlight the prestige of the position. It is a huge privilege to be appointed as a QC and is the dream for many barristers, including barristers who are as new to the profession as me! Silks take on the most high-profile, complex cases and are the barristers who represent clients in the highest courts. They are usually accompanied by another barrister during these cases, who again will be referred to as a 'junior' no matter how senior they are. QCs also tend to charge higher fees than ordinary barristers, in recognition of their expertise.

The profession is still immersed in tradition. The title 'Queen's Counsel' refers directly to the current monarch. If the monarch changes to a king, the titles will change accordingly to King's Counsel (KC). Newly appointed QCs[2] are invited to a ceremony in which they must dress in elaborate legal clothing that makes the entire event look like a period drama. There is a frilly white collar and frilly white cuffs on the sleeves. The new silks also have white gloves, which most seem to just hold in their hands. The wigs are also longer and resemble a cocker spaniel's ears as they are curly and flop on either side of the head.

For the moment, though, I was content with my short barrister's wig. Being a pupil barrister was difficult enough.

I struggled to explain to my friends and family how tough my profession could be. I was learning to deal with the fact that sometimes my client, who I was trying my best to help, would lie to my face. There were lots of cases

---

[2] There are just over 100 Queen's Counsel appointments every year. In 2019, there were 114 appointments. In the previous three years the numbers were 108 (2018), 119 (2017) and 113 (2016). https://www.qcappointments.org

like Mr Noah's where my clients seemed to do everything in their power to undermine the chances of success. Sometimes I felt that, despite my best efforts, I couldn't make the difference I wanted to.

On my toughest days I thought about Ayo and I remembered why I started this journey. He didn't get the chance to fulfil his dreams, but here I was with the chance to live mine and I knew I couldn't take that for granted. I remembered why I started this journey. I had to contextualise the difficult moments: I had helped to protect clients from abusive ex-partners and I'd ensured other clients were acquitted of the crimes they had been wrongfully charged with. I was proud to be ensuring that defendants were tried fairly within our legal system, no matter what their background. In all of my cases, I had supported people (innocent or guilty), through some of the most challenging days of their lives.

8

Being Black

I was nervous for my first case in the Crown Court. I was representing Mr Ahmed, who was charged with possession of drugs with intent to supply (a large amount of cannabis). Whilst I had dealt with many drug cases in the Magistrates' Court before, judges in the Crown Court have greater sentencing powers (they aren't limited to a six-month custodial sentence per offence) and this weighed heavily on my mind. My client could face a substantial amount of time in prison and he was only 18 years old. I was being trusted by my client and his solicitor with a serious case where my client's liberty was undoubtedly on the line.

Rushing into the robing room to put on my wig and gown, I bumped into a senior barrister I knew who invited me to join his conversation with a colleague. They were discussing the judge we were all due to appear in front of that day. As usual, we started to work out how likely we were to succeed in our cases based on what we had heard from others about the judge. We concluded that the judge was very fair and balanced and whatever decision he reached would likely be the most appropriate, even if it was unfavourable to our respective clients.

The barrister I hadn't met before turned to me and smiled, delighted with our conclusions. He paused, took a breath and declared, 'At least the racist judge has retired. I've got a black kid today and he would have had no hope.'

I glanced at him, unsure of how to react.

He added, 'It's a huge relief for black boys everywhere that he's gone.'

I lowered my head and thought about what he'd said. It was true, I guess. If a 'racist' judge had retired, that was a brilliant thing for everyone, 'black boys' particularly. It worried me that it had been so normalised that there were judges who were perceived to be racist. I didn't get the opportunity to ask this barrister any further questions but, based on what I had been told, I was concerned that it seemed that it had been accepted that it was just 'the way the judge was'.

Mr Ahmed was a young black man on the cusp of being sent to prison. His mitigation – that is, the factors that were relevant to the court reducing any sentence – covered multiple pages of my notebook. My instructing solicitor had known him since he was a young child when he had started to get involved in criminal activity. One thing was clear, this young man's life would not be helped by being sent to prison.

Most young people caught up in the criminal justice system are struggling with financial issues, often living in poverty. Mr Ahmed was unemployed and didn't have any family to support him financially or otherwise; he had spent the vast majority of his childhood in the care system. Whilst I was relieved that a 'racist judge' had left, I remained concerned about the fate of my client. Black men, like Mr Ahmed, are overrepresented in the youth and adult justice system.[1] The guidelines given to magistrates and judges sentencing young people[2] suggest that they should be aware that a significant proportion of looked after children are from BAME backgrounds.[3] Magistrates and judges are advised to recognise how being in the care system might have affected these young people when sentencing them, as there is a correlation between this and rates of offending in young people – in other words, children in care commit more criminal offences

---

[1] 'Black, Asian and Minority Ethnic disproportionality in the Criminal Justice System in England and Wales', Ministry of Justice. For example, black individuals account for about 3 per cent of the total population of England and Wales yet make up about 9 per cent of defendants prosecuted for indictable offences. https://www.gov.uk/government/uploads/system/uploads/attachment_data/file/568680/bame-disproportionality-in-the-cjs.pdf

[2] https://www.sentencingcouncil.org.uk/overarching-guides/magistrates-court/item/sentencing-children-and-young-people/

[3] 23 per cent of children in foster care in 2018 were from non-white ethnic minority groups. https://www.gov.uk/government/publications/fostering-in-england-1-april-2017-to-31-march-2018/fostering-in-england-2017-to-2018-main-findings

proportionally.[4] Many looked after children have little or no contact with their family or have had to relocate a number of times which is likely to have had an impact on their wellbeing. In addition, in the care system, a child is statistically more likely to be exposed to others who are offending or who have previously offended.

Another important factor, one that I could see in Mr Ahmed's case, is that many BAME young people experience discrimination and have negative experiences of authority. Some of this discrimination manifests in the way that they are treated by law enforcement, but also arises as early as school where many BAME children, especially black students, are treated unfairly.[5] Mr Ahmed had struggled with authority, having been excluded from multiple schools.

Mr Ahmed told me that he felt that the system was against him. I could hear the frustration and upset in his voice. 'I just feel like everyone is against me. I feel like that judge is just going to look at me and think, "Oh, another drug

---

[4] In 2013, 6.1 per cent of looked after children between 10 and 17 years old had been convicted or subject to a final warning or reprimand during the year. This compares with 1.2 per cent of all children in this age group in the same year. https://assets. publishing.service.gov.uk/government/uploads/system/uploads/attachment_ data/file/384781/Outcomes_SFR49_2014_Text.pdf

[5] Non-black teachers can have lower expectations of black students (Gershenson, Holt, & Papageorge, 2016; Gillborn, Rollock, Vincent and Ball, 2012), and are more likely to negatively judge (such as discipline or label) pupils from minority ethnic backgrounds (Hattie, 2009). https://cfey.org/wp-content/uploads/2018/12/ LKMco-and-GLA-Boys-on-Track-FINAL-version-for-web.pdf

dealer". I don't want this to be my life, man.'

He looked up at the ceiling and closed his eyes. He sat still for a few moments, inhaling and exhaling slowly. Then he spoke again: 'Look. I was just trying to make some money. I don't have qualifications; I don't have a family. I don't have anyone…'

Mr Ahmed looked surprised that I agreed with him that the system was not in his favour. He said he was tired of constantly trying to argue with people who told him that it was all about his life choices. I reassured him that I would do my utmost to ensure that the court was aware of all of the circumstances around his offending behaviour. I told him that I'd spoken to his solicitor who had confirmed that the details I'd been given about his background were correct, thereby preventing him having to retell his traumatic childhood to yet another stranger.

'Mr Ahmed, I'm on your side.'

He lifted his gaze and looked me in the eye. A small smile appeared on his face. 'Thank you. No one ever listens.'

In court, I laid out all of the mitigating factors about my client for the judge's consideration. He paused and thanked me before turning to my client and asking him to stand.

'You were found in possession of a substantial amount of cannabis, almost half a kilo. I acknowledge that you have taken responsibility and pleaded at the earliest opportunity. You played a significant role in this offending and I put this

IN BLACK AND WHITE

offence in category three of the sentencing guidelines. That gives me a starting point of one year of custody, with a range of six months up to three years. I note that you have previous convictions but they are not relevant to this offence. I also note that you are just 18 years old and I have taken into consideration everything that Ms Wilson has said about your very difficult personal circumstances.'

I felt nervous as the judge got closer to giving my client his sentence. I couldn't see Mr Ahmed as he was in the dock behind me but I imagined him fidgeting, as he had done when I explained that he may be facing a custodial sentence.

'Mr Ahmed,' the judge continued. 'I would have given you a 12-month sentence but I have reduced this to 8 months to reflect your early guilty plea.'

I heard sniffling behind me but the judge had not yet finished. 'I am suspending this sentence for a period of 18 months. In that time, you will be on a community order. You will complete a Thinking Skills Programme for 20 days.' (This was a group work programme designed to help prevent Mr Ahmed from re-offending.)

The judge continued: 'You will also complete a Rehabilitation Activity Requirement for ten days.' The RAR meant that Mr Ahmed's probation officer would help him choose courses adding up to a certain number of hours, aimed at developing the skills he needed to function in the community, reducing the chance he would reoffend.

The judge warned Mr Ahmed that any breach of these conditions would bring him back before the court. He ordered that the seized drugs be destroyed and that Mr Ahmed pay a victim surcharge.

Mr Ahmed was pleased with the judge's decision. I rang his solicitor who was delighted that he had avoided a custodial sentence. We both agreed that nothing would have been achieved by sending him to prison and at least these programmes would give him a chance, hopefully providing him with the support he needed to tackle some of the issues that he was struggling with.

* * *

Theresa May, the former prime minister, acknowledged the racial disparities in the criminal justice system in her first speech in office on 13 July 2016. She said, 'If you're black, you're treated more harshly by the criminal justice system than if you're white.'[6]

The *Independent* newspaper investigated racial disparities in sentencing in England and Wales using data from 2009 to 2017. They found that one in four black teenagers convicted of manslaughter were given maximum custodial sentences (a 'life' sentence) but no white teenager was sentenced to more than 10 years. The majority of white teenagers (over 50 per

[6] https://www.gov.uk/government/speeches/statement-from-the-new-prime-minister-theresa-may

cent) received less than four years, whereas only 5 per cent of black teenagers received a sentence of less than four years.[7]

During the same period – 2009 to 2017 – 73 black teenagers were found guilty of murder or manslaughter. Black teenagers were far more likely than white teenagers to be convicted of murder, which carries a mandatory life sentence. The majority (over 50 per cent) of the 102 white teenagers tried during that period were convicted of manslaughter rather than murder, compared with just 30 per cent of black teenagers.

Part of this disparity in sentencing might be explained by an entrenched mistrust of the system among ethnic minority communities, leading to an unwillingness to plead guilty and, as a result, being less likely to receive credit – a shorter sentence, essentially – for a guilty plea. Statistics produced by the Ministry of Justice showed that black, Asian and other ethnic minority men were at least 50 per cent more likely than white men to plead not guilty at the Crown Court.[8]

Entering a guilty plea can make a real difference to the sentence a person will receive. If a defendant pleads guilty at the earliest opportunity (that is, the first time they appear in

---

[7] https://www.independent.co.uk/news/uk/home-news/black-boys-discrimination-teenagers-children-white-racial-bias-prison-a8466606.html

[8] https://assets.publishing.service.gov.uk/government/uploads/system/uploads/attachment_data/file/639261/bame-disproportionality-in-the-cjs.pdf

court) then they will receive up to a third discount on their final sentence. If, in Crown Court cases, the defendant only pleads at the Plea and Trial Preparation Hearing (PTPH), then they will only receive up to a 25 per cent reduction on their sentence. This is to reflect the fact that more time and resources have gone into the case.

Finally, if a person decides to plead on the day of trial (stopping it from going ahead), they will receive a comparatively small sentence reduction of up to 10 per cent. If someone is facing a long sentence, this can make a huge difference. So a comparison between pleading guilty at the earliest opportunity, and changing to a guilty plea on the day of the trail, gives a significant difference in jail terms that minority defendants appear to be losing out on.

One explanation of the lack of trust that a lot of my black clients have in the legal system as a whole is that they are more likely to be arrested or charged with an offence than their white peers. My client, Mr Ahmed, had expressed this frustration. He experienced frequent harassment from the police but none of his white friends who sold drugs were ever stopped. According to a 2013 report by the charity Release, despite black people being found to be less likely to use drugs than white people, they were twice as likely to be charged with drug possession.[9]

---

[9] https://www.release.org.uk/publications/numbers-black-and-white-ethnic-disparities-policing-and-prosecution-drug-offences

I am not surprised by the findings of the report. My brothers and male friends were harassed by police whilst we were growing up. My brother, dressed in his smart suit, would often be stopped on the way to work in Essex and asked questions by officers. My friends, dressed for a day of work in the City would also be stopped and told they matched a reported suspect. When asked what that description was, they were only ever told that the description was of a black (or, sometimes more coldly, an 'IC3') male. They felt harassed. It's hardly surprising that many of these young people do not feel that the police are there to protect them.

* * *

My grandparents came to the UK from Jamaica as part of the Windrush generation. They came to help 'rebuild Britain' after the Second World War, the country they were told was theirs. My grandfather worked multiple jobs, including being a postman. He was the best cook in the world. Like most children I hated vegetables, but my grandad had a way of steaming seasoned sweet potato, carrots and yam and making them taste as good to my childhood taste buds as candyfloss. My grandmother was a nurse and my memories of her are of a proud woman who taught me that a woman can be just as powerful, intelligent and successful as a man.

My grandparents were treated with hostility when they came to the UK. They suffered racial abuse. My grandad used to tell me stories about the signs in the windows of B&Bs and houses to rent, that read 'No blacks'. He made me appreciate how much of a blessing it was that I was born to such loving parents who were white and black, despite the difficult racial tensions still existing in our country.

My uncle Pat was born in Jamaica and came to England with my grandparents when he was a young child. He was a Rastafarian and I have fond memories of playing with his beautiful and impressive dreadlocks. His long-term partner, Aunty Sue, was also white, like my mum. My uncle had sickle-cell anaemia and as a late teen he was in a car accident in which he lost a lot of blood. The result was that he was then wheelchair-bound. When I was young my aunt and uncle would look after me. They were close to my parents. Uncle Pat was the best man at my parent's wedding.

In November 1982, over ten years before I was born, my uncle had dropped my aunt off at work and was driving home to Nunhead where they lived together when he was stopped by the police for allegedly possessing drugs. The five police officers asked my uncle to get out of the car, to which he explained that he was a wheelchair user and could not. At this point, they began to be verbally abusive to my uncle and assaulted him.

My uncle, understandably, was scared. I don't remember

him as a fearful person but the situation must have been terrifying. He was a disabled man who had done nothing wrong. The officers were making racially abusive comments and he was afraid of what might happen next. He decided to turn his car around and drove back to the taxi office where my aunt worked so that he would have a witness with him. The officers followed.

Aunty Sue told me how she pleaded with the officers to leave my uncle alone and explained that he was not being defiant. He was disabled and had a wheelchair in the back of the car. The officers were uninterested in what she said and arrested both of them in what can only be described as an inhumane way. Both my uncle and aunt were assaulted multiple times on arrest and again on the way to the police station. My uncle was dropped onto the floor inside the police van. My aunt was forced to strip and jump up and down naked.

The officers tried to allege that my aunt and uncle were in possession of drugs. No drugs were found on my aunt. No drugs were found on my uncle. No drugs were found in my uncle's car, which was impounded. There were no drugs.

My aunt and uncle sued the Metropolitan Police. They challenged the assault, the false imprisonment and the subsequent malicious prosecution.

In December 1985, their case was heard at the Old Bailey. The judge, Sir David Tudor Price, said that the police had been 'disgraceful' and behaved 'oppressively and in abuse of their powers'.

It was reported in *The Times* on 17 December, by Bernard Levin, who wrote: 'Mr Wilson had been unlawfully arrested, maliciously prosecuted, falsely imprisoned, and for good measure assaulted, and that Miss Farbridge had been unlawfully arrested, falsely imprisoned and likewise (and humiliatingly) assaulted.'[10]

He added: 'If five officers conspire to commit unlawful arrest, malicious prosecution, false imprisonment and assault on a black man and his white companion, and then lie themselves even deeper into the mire while their superiors, who can see a barn door by daylight, are striving to prevent the case coming to court, then it seems to me that there is something very much deeper and rottener at the heart of the Met than the inevitable incidence of a few bad and dishonest members of it.'

On 6 December 1985, my aunt and uncle were awarded damages as 'a mark of disapproval against the police', according to *The Times*. The damages weren't a significant amount of money, and my aunt and uncle weren't particularly interested in the money anyway, but they were pleased that the courts were able to hold the police to account.

---

[10] 'Who Will Defend Us Against the Bullies in Blue?' *The Times*, 17 December 1985

My uncle's story is heart-breaking, and both my uncle and aunt continued to have a deep mistrust of the police after this very traumatising incident. The money was a token gesture in that it recognised that they had been mistreated but it didn't change what had been done. The court was able to bring them a sense of justice, however. The words of the judge were important as it showed them that the law applies equally to everyone, including the police. My uncle and aunt's experience influenced my decision to become a barrister. While the law could not undo wrongs, it could offer some relief to those who had suffered. When I was growing up, I remember my family talking about institutional racism in the police and the Stephen Lawrence Inquiry. This was a landmark public inquiry into the death of a black, 18-year-old boy called Stephen Lawrence, who was murdered in a racially motivated attack in Eltham, south-east London in 1993. The report concluded that the Metropolitan Police's investigation into Stephen's death had been incompetent. The police officers had made significant failures such as not administering first aid at the scene; ignoring leads and not arresting suspects. Most significantly, the report concluded that the Metropolitan Police were 'institutionally racist'.

As children, my generation were told stories by our parents and other family members about the harassment and the abuse that they received from police officers.

After the results of the Stephen Lawrence inquiry were published in early 1999, we could then read in the news, or learn on the internet, that what we'd been told had been officially confirmed – the police *were* racist. Whilst things do seem to have improved, largely because of better diversity in the police, I think it's hardly surprising that many black people have an inherent distrust of the authorities. There is still a substantial amount of work to be done in rebuilding trust in black and other ethnic minority communities.

A significant part of institutional racism is unconscious bias; these are the social stereotypes about groups of people that we form without realising. In a speech titled 'Fairness in the Courts: The Best We Can Do', Lord Neuberger, then president of the Supreme Court, acknowledged that '[t]he big problem, as it is everywhere, is with unconscious bias. I dare say that we all suffer from a degree of unconscious bias, and it can occur in all sorts of manifestations.'

He explained: 'A white male public school judge presiding in a trial of an unemployed traveller from Eastern Europe accused of assaulting or robbing a white female public school woman will, I hope, always been [sic] unbiased. However, he should always think to himself what his subconscious may be thinking or how it may be causing him to act; and he should always remember how things may look to the defendant, and indeed to the jury and to the public generally.'[11]

Whilst judges might have unconscious biases, there also appears to be unconscious bias in the selection of judges: only 7 per cent of court judges are from a BAME background.[12] To date, I have never seen a black male judge in any of the cases that I have observed or acted in. Anecdotally, many barristers explain that this is because historically the Bar (where most judges are recruited from) was overwhelmingly white but, as the Lord Chief Justice recognised almost 30 years ago, this reason is 'ceasing to be valid' given that so many ethnic minorities have entered the profession and have reached the point of being eligible for appointment.[13] The first black barrister was Christian Cole (who was also the first black graduate from Oxford and coincidentally went to University College, Oxford, like me). He was admitted to Inner Temple in 1879 and called to the Bar in 1883. The first black judge appears to have been Tunji Sowande who became the first black deputy circuit judge (assistant recorder) in 1978. The first black Queen's

---

[11] https://www.supremecourt.uk/docs/speech-150410.pdf

[12] https://www.judiciary.uk/about-the-judiciary/who-are-the-judiciary/diversity/judicial-diversity-statistics-2019/

[13] Lord Taylor, *The Judiciary in the Nineties*, Richard Dimbleby Lecture, 1992, cited in House of Lords, Select Committee on the Constitution, *Judicial Appointments*, 25th Report of Session 2010–12, note 132, available online at https://www.publications.parliament.uk/pa/ld201012/ldselect/ldconst/272/272.pdf

Counsel, Dr John Roberts QC, wasn't appointed until ten years later, in 1988.

It is difficult to show how slow the pace of change is with statistics because the data only shows the number of BAME barristers that are pupils, juniors or QCs. However, the fact that it took almost 100 years from the first black barrister being called to the Bar to the first black judge being appointed, and even longer for the first black QC to be appointed, demonstrates how slow the profession has been to improve ethnic diversity.

Justice (a law reform and human rights organisation in the UK) published a report in which it recognised that the public might question the legitimacy and objectivity of judicial judgments made by an 'overwhelmingly white, male and privately educated judiciary'.[14] The report emphasised that the quality of the senior judiciary would improve when judges are drawn from a more diverse background and offered two further explanations as to why BAME people are underrepresented in the judiciary.

One reason given is that eligible people from BAME backgrounds don't put themselves forward. However, the Judicial Appointments Commission's statistics show that when BAME people apply for judicial appointments, they are much less likely to be successful

---

[14] https://justice.org.uk/wp-content/uploads/2017/04/JUSTICE-Increasing-judicial-diversity-report-2017-web.pdf

than their white peers.[15] In any event, if people from BAME backgrounds are not applying, this reflects badly on the judicial appointments system. It reflects a culture that does not feel welcoming to BAME lawyers and it's made more difficult by the fact that there are relatively few current BAME judges to mentor those from the same groups who wish to become judges. It is clear to me that more needs to be done to actively encourage BAME lawyers who are eligible to apply for judicial positions but also to support them in that application process.

Another popular excuse is that judges are appointed on merit. The implication being that merit and diversity are mutually exclusive. The report published by Justice found that, contrary to these concerns, 'achieving the highest quality judiciary *requires* more women, BAME people and greater social diversity'. It is difficult to assess how many BAME barristers are eligible for appointment. Some suggest that because the Bar has been slow to adequately represent BAME barristers, there are not enough BAME barristers of the required level to appoint a diverse judiciary. The statistics do not currently give a clear enough picture

---

[15] For example, 22 per cent of applications were by BAME lawyers, yet only 14 per cent were successfully recommended for judicial positions. In fact, the JAC statistics note that the recommendation rates for BAME applicants is lower than for white applicants across all exercises combined. The exercises are assessed tasks that applicants have to engage in as part of the recruitment process.

in terms of the number of BAME barristers over 40 years old (the age most judges are appointed after). This clearly warrants further investigation.

On one occasion, I was confronted by a barrister in the robing room who insisted on telling me that the 'diversity drive' in the judiciary is having a negative effect on the quality of judges. This barrister was relatively old, I would estimate that he was in his late sixties, but that, in my opinion, was no excuse for his ignorance. I hadn't even invited this conversation; I was merely typing up my attendance note for my solicitor when he plonked himself next to me and began to speak to me. He told me, explicitly, that he thought ethnic minority barristers and solicitors were being promoted to the judiciary to help the judiciary meet targets and look good but they weren't of the same quality as judges previously appointed. I was confused as to why he thought he needed to share that opinion with me. There were three other people in the robing room and I didn't know this man. However, the others were white men and I was led to the obvious conclusion that he felt that he could best offload his grievances to a young, ethnic minority woman.

Worse still, his confidence grew as I silently listened to him tell me that things have changed for the worst. He leant back in his chair and his voice grew in volume. A younger, white male joined the conversation and agreed that the 'old system' was better. I had expected him to delve into how the system was 'fairer' but to my surprise he advocated for the way it used to be done, when people would 'get a tap on the shoulder' and be told to apply to be a judge. I couldn't understand why anyone in their right mind would think that this was a sensible system.

Their conversation only finished when I stood up to leave. I began to question how much more ignorance I could take from individuals within my own profession; these two barristers would be representing people from a diverse range of backgrounds but were expressing such prejudice behind closed doors. However, as much as this experience got me down, I knew there were plenty of good people practising law, too. My tenancy decision was months away; I couldn't quit now. I was determined to be the change I wanted to see. I wasn't going to let anyone stop me.

9

Children in Court

It was 9.45am and I was impatiently pacing up and down on the shrivelled, off-green carpets of the waiting area in the youth court, looking for my client. As usual, I had only received the case the evening before and had never met the person I was about to be representing. I hate the game of 'guess the client' because you end up asking 20 people if they are your client and they all return a blank stare and a resounding no. In the past I've had clients who have been everywhere but the courtroom: shopping because they forgot they had to be in court; in the police station because they've been arrested for something else; at home because they can't be bothered; or in prison because the prison van mixed up the names and didn't bring my client to court.

Most barristers might have the benefit of the client being able to recognise them from the professional photo on their chambers' website but pupil barristers are often not given that privilege. Any client who googles you will either see all your holiday photographs (a good reason to have your personal social media on private) or, if you have a similar name to another barrister, will be expecting someone entirely different to show up. They often have little or no idea of who will be representing them on one of the most important days of their lives.

However, in the youth courts (which deal with children between the ages of 10 and 17) it is even harder to find your client. The names of children appearing is not on the public court list and youth court proceedings aren't in the public domain. This is because young people's identities have to be protected, and so you can hardly shout your client's name out across the whole waiting area without undermining the principal rule of confidentiality. The cases are conducted in private so even other barristers and solicitors cannot sit at the back of the courtroom whilst youth proceedings are going on. The anonymity of youth court proceedings is a step towards recognising that young people are vulnerable and legal proceedings can be daunting and have a life-long impact.

So, in short, finding the young person I am supposed to be representing in court in a matter of minutes is challenging, to say the least. It's unlikely that they will try to find me by questioning every adult in the waiting area. Sometimes the parents will enquire, as every child under the age of 16 must attend court with an appropriate adult (usually a parent or guardian), but many do not. In the interests of preserving privacy, I am often forced to narrow down who my client might be based only on their name, age and the 'helpful' descriptions set out in any witness statements that are given to me either the night before or that same day.

Some of the descriptions of clients are frankly hilarious. I have been on the lookout for a client who was 'average height, average build, brown hair and white'. I was expected to find them with no further descriptors. In family law cases (unlike in criminal cases), I rarely know what my client will look like. In criminal cases a witness might include physical descriptions of the defendant in their statement, in case the defendant denies being the person who committed the offence. In family cases there is no need for the parties to include a physical description – both parties know each other and hence there are no issues in relation to identity. The only time I've ever had a clue is if the client says she was called a 'white X' or a 'black Y' or a 'skinny Z', etc. by an ex-partner, when describing abuse she has suffered.

On one occasion, I had no physical description of my client to go by other than the fact that she had 'wonky eyes', as noted by the police officer. Not only did this make me stare into the eyes of every person who came into the court building but I also had to explain to my client (who had not previously seen the statements) that being described as having 'wonky eyes' was not something to worry about. For at least 15 minutes of our valuable conference time, my client repeatedly stated that she did not have 'wonky eyes', she was just able to look in two different directions at one time. I nodded reassuringly and tried to move the conversation on but the description did nothing but hinder me being able to take her instructions.

I knew very little about today's client, Layla, other than the fact that she was female and 14 years old. The witness statements described her as being somewhere between five and six feet tall (helpful) and having either blonde or brown hair (even more helpful).

My instructing solicitors had told me that this was a potential 'county lines' case. 'County lines' is a term that has been widely used in the newspapers. It refers to an organised criminal network exploiting young and vulnerable people by sending them to sell drugs in rural areas. The young people involved are instructed to travel across counties (the 'county' part) and use basic, hard-to-trace phones (the 'lines' part) to supply drugs. The Children's Commissioner estimates that there are at least 46,000 children in England involved in gang activity and about 4,000 in London alone are being exploited through county lines activity.[1]

The perpetrators of county lines offences are typically older gang members who profit from the sales generated

---

[1] https://www.childrenssociety.org.uk/what-is-county-lines

by these drug operations. The Modern Slavery Act 2015 clearly sets out that there is exploitation where a person arranges or facilitates the travel of children or vulnerable adults for them to sell sex, firearms or drugs.

Layla had been arrested for being involved in the supply of class B drugs. She claimed that she had never sold cannabis, but just had it for personal use. She told me that she didn't have to pay for it because her 'friends' gave it to her for free. The police report detailed that when she was arrested, she had £100 in cash, which they deemed unusual for a girl of her age. The police officer also commented on how 'unwashed' she looked. He remarked how attached Layla was to her phone. He noted that during the arrest Layla received a stream of messages asking where she was.

I now regularly represent young people in cases like this; it makes up about 25 per cent of my criminal practice. These children are driven out to the countryside by or on the instructions of older 'friends' who tell them that they will protect them. They are made to operate drug sales from a stranger's home, which has been taken over by the gang. This has become known as 'cuckooing' and often involves the exploitation of a vulnerable homeowner – often people with learning difficulties – in these rural counties.

When children are dealing drugs there are always

more questions to be asked. They are often subjected to violence and sexual exploitation. As the awareness of county lines drug dealing has grown so has the understanding of the safeguards that need to be in place to ensure that young people are not unfairly prosecuted. There is guidance for prosecutors on how young people might have a defence if the Home Office finds that they are a victim of child exploitation.

However, I don't think the safeguards that exist currently are sufficient because the Crown Prosecution Service (CPS), the body responsible for prosecutions that have been investigated by the police in England and Wales, do not always take a holistic view of the offending behaviour. In some of my cases, the CPS decided that the exploitation of the child began on a specific date and hence any offending behaviour that took place before that did not arise out of exploitation. And yet these issues cannot be handled so narrowly because child exploitation is rarely something that happens suddenly overnight. Many of the children are groomed for a substantial period of time and the amount of pressure placed on them gradually increases.

I knew that Layla's social worker had made a referral for Layla to be assessed to decide whether or not she would be considered a victim of child exploitation but I didn't know whether there had been any other update.

Layla was supposed to meet me at 9am but there was

no one in the court who fitted the loose description I had. I dialled the solicitor's number and left a second message, praying that someone would call me back. It was now 10am and the court usher was welcoming the first case into court. She warned me that the court would expect an update on my case in 10 minutes. I looked at the usher with wide eyes that communicated an 'I'm really trying' message and the usher reassured me that she would try to buy me some time. I smiled gratefully and headed over to the Youth Offending Team's (YOT) room. YOT provide support for young people and encourage them to stay away from criminal activity or behaviour. They run programmes for young people on matters such as weapons awareness and anger management and they supervise them when they are serving a community sentence.

There was a queue outside the office – a stream of black-suit-clad barristers and solicitors all trying to locate missing reports and information in an attempt to hurry their cases along the extensive youth court list. Many of these barristers were likely to have another case in the afternoon in a court at least an hour away (like I did). Given the abysmal pay for so many of these cases, there's a real incentive to try and deal with each case as efficiently as humanly possible. I recognised a few people in the queue, other pupil barristers.

It strikes me how strange it is that the freshest people and most inexperienced in the profession (pupil barristers) are expected to represent youths, one of the most vulnerable groups in our society. The Bar Standards Board recently introduced a requirement that anyone conducting cases in the youth court must self-certify to say that they have received training in the specialist skills, knowledge and attributes necessary to work effectively with young people. The problem is that there is no compulsory training for youth court work. My chambers were willing to pay for me to take part in youth justice training run by the Youth Justice Legal Centre (YJLC), prior to me doing any youth court work, but not all pupil barristers have this opportunity and the courses are a few hundred pounds, which can be a substantial sum for a trainee barrister.

The training run by YJLC is excellent and should be compulsory for all barristers. It comprised scenario-based exercises and expert lectures on current issues facing children in the criminal justice system; for example, we had a session that focused on recognising county lines cases. Most significantly, the training included role play exercises with young people, which gave them the opportunity to give us advice on how we interact with our young clients in conferences before and after court. We were privileged to listen to a talk by a man who had served time in prison for attempted murder as a child about how incarceration had affected him and his family and friends.

He spoke about how difficult it is to be locked up at such a young age and talked about the negative impact that it had on his mental health.

My youth court case was listed in a courtroom with nine other cases, which meant that at least nine young people were expected to take the day off from school that morning. Many parents also had to take a day off work to accompany their children and some had arrived dressed in their Sunday best, recognising the formality of the courts. I could see in the waiting area that a number of young people were accompanied by social workers sporting lanyards but some children appeared to be sitting alone. It was strange to see so many young people in one place, all looking so sombre.

After what felt like an eternity, the Youth Offending Team welcomed me into their closet-like office. I explained my desperation – my solicitor was not answering the phone and my vulnerable client, Layla, was nowhere to be seen. The man behind the desk had short afro hair that was balding in the centre. He chuckled light-heartedly and teased me for being so worried when there were so many cases in the list. He swivelled his chair to face the large desktop computer and tapped ferociously at the keyboard. The clock hanging on the wall ticked loudly but the hands didn't move. Time was frozen on this broken clock and it was strangely comforting.

While waiting for him to find Layla's contact details, I asked whether he had any update on the referral that Layla's social worker had made. He said that the Home Office had decided that there were 'reasonable grounds' to believe that she was a victim of child exploitation. Given this decision, the Home Office were now proceeding to investigate her case more fully and to decide whether (on the balance of probabilities) she was a victim of child exploitation. This meant that today we would be asking for an adjournment, awaiting the Home Office's final decision.

The man dialled the contact number he had found for Layla. He briefly explained to the person on the other end of the phone, who I assumed was her mother, that Layla was supposed to be in court at 9am and asked where she was. There was clearly a lack of response from the other side because the man's tone softened as he asked her mother whether she could understand English. More silence followed as we waited. A minute passed. Then another.

Although it was a weekday, I knew Layla wouldn't be at school. She had been in many schools and had recently been excluded from her pupil referral unit[2] so was no longer in education. This is often the case for many young

---

[2] A pupil referral unit is an alternative education provision for children who cannot attend mainstream schools, one of the main reasons for this is that they have been excluded from mainstream education.

people in the criminal justice system, who have bounced between schools and pupil referral units for much of their childhood. In a Ministry of Justice survey conducted in 2012, 63 per cent of adult prisoners had been suspended or temporarily excluded from school and 42 per cent said they had been permanently excluded or expelled.[3]

These statistics are hardly surprising when you consider the impact of an exclusion: children don't only miss out on formal education but also on the social aspect of school. It can be very difficult to return to mainstream school once a child has been permanently excluded; children who have been excluded from other schools are not the most desirable students and schools will often find a multitude of reasons as to why they cannot accept them. It can become even more difficult when a child has not only been permanently excluded from mainstream schools but then excluded from a pupil referral unit, or even multiple units. These children sometimes end up at home with no schooling at all.

The man in the YOT office started to stare at the ceiling and tapped his fingers on his desk in time with the broken clock. I lifted up my wrist to check the time on my own watch. It was creeping up to 11am. The man started speaking again and it was clear from his tone that he was now talking to Layla. He asked whether she had

---

[3] https://assets.publishing.service.gov.uk/government/uploads/system/uploads/attachment_data/file/278837/prisoners-childhood-family-backgrounds.pdf

just woken up. The conversation continued briefly as he reminded her that she was supposed to be in court. He asked her how long it might take to get to court and when the answer finally came, he didn't sound happy. He let out a huge sigh and closed his eyes for a few seconds. He sternly told her to be as quick as she could and ended the call. The man turned back to me and unexpectedly chuckled. He confirmed my interpretation. Layla had just woken up and wouldn't arrive for at least two hours.

One of the most frustrating things about this job is the waiting around, particularly because most of the time we don't get paid for it. The waiting time adds up and there is rarely somewhere you can sit down and focus on getting some work done. Most of the advocates' rooms are small and even if they do have a table, there are usually a limited number of chairs. While we are waiting, we have to be careful not to open confidential papers or write about another case on our laptops in public waiting areas so we are fairly restricted in what we can do to fill the dead time. On the days when I have the most waiting time, I always forget to bring a book and so I end up scrolling through social media and reading the news. I never look forward to the waiting time.

Two hours later, just before the court lunch hour, Layla arrived. She strolled into court and asked the security guards where her lawyer was. I'd spent the last couple of hours catching up on some admin and revisiting the case notes in a lonely corner of the waiting area, using my brand-new laptop privacy screen. I'd headed over to the front entrance of the court about 10 minutes beforehand, anticipating that she would arrive soon. I could see her social worker following her closely behind. I introduced myself and led her into a conference room.

Layla had no interest in going through the evidence in any detail and I explained that today would be largely administrative; we would be asking for the case to be adjourned pending the Home Office's decision. Although barely engaged she nodded along to what I was saying. Her phone rang repeatedly throughout our conference and I asked her to turn it off, which she pretended to do but I saw that she merely put it on silent mode. She kept asking when we would be done. We finished the conference and returned to the waiting area with her social worker.

Layla, sitting in front of me with her legs up on the waiting area seats, had a brand-new phone. I asked her when she got it.

'Last week. Social services got it for me,' she said, not looking up.

The social worker shook her head and leaned towards me to whisper: 'We didn't. We're concerned about where Layla is getting all of these new things.'

The social worker went on to tell me that social services

were worried about Layla spending a lot of her time with men in their twenties; the people she was calling her 'friends'. The social worker suspected that the gifts were provided by them and had her suspicions as to what was expected in return. Every night Layla disappeared for hours and would return in the early hours of the morning or sometimes wouldn't come home for a few days.

I looked at Layla again. She was wearing brand-new trainers and a coat that I knew cost at least a few hundred pounds.

A major difficulty for anyone working with these young people is that they often don't believe that they are being exploited and feel that they are in control of their circumstances. The people exploiting these teenagers often draw them in by showing them large amounts of money, nice clothes, expensive cars and what might seem like an otherwise unattainable lifestyle to a child living in poverty.

I invited Layla back into a conference room to talk. She was reluctant but followed me in. I asked her whether the older boys she had befriended were buying her these items. She giggled nervously and looked away. I waited patiently. She said that they were. I asked whether they were the same people that gave her drugs. She shrugged.

'Layla, do they give you drugs to sell?'

Layla's face went white and she stared at me coldly.

'You don't understand. I can't tell you anything. Please ask them to put me on tag. They come and pick me up in the evenings. Just, please, I want to just be put on a tag so I just can't go out.'

I was shocked. I had never had a client who had asked to be electronically monitored. It made sense. She wanted to be able to say no to her 'friends' but didn't know how to; a tag would keep her indoors in the evening. I explained that pleading guilty was unlikely to lead to her being put on an electronic tag. Given that the Home Office was assessing whether she was a victim of child exploitation, today's hearing would just be adjourned awaiting the Home Office's decision, which could take up to six months (but sometimes takes longer). My client nodded but didn't say anything.

The case was adjourned, successfully. I spoke to Layla, her mother and the social worker. Her mother could not speak much English but had tears in her eyes as she asked me whether these 'bad people', who Layla was spending time with, would be stopped. I tried to explain that the Home Office were continuing to investigate whether or not Layla was a victim of child exploitation. There was little more that I could say. After what I had heard I could only hope that Layla was willing to talk openly to the person carrying out the assessment. I encouraged her to be forthcoming about everything, as difficult as that would be. I knew I was unlikely to see her again as I was covering this case last minute for someone else. I could see that she was terrified. All I could do was urge her to put a small amount of faith into the system; a system that she had no reason to trust. I quickly learned that this is the reality for young and vulnerable people in our criminal justice system.

* * *

The most memorable cases are not always the most serious ones; some cases stick out in my mind because they should not have been in court. On a number of occasions I've represented children brought to court for offences that could have been dealt with differently.

Sarah was 13 years old and suffered with a number of learning difficulties. She attended court with her father for smashing an interactive white board in her school. Sarah looked even younger than her age. She had curly brown hair that covered her eyes as she leaned forwards and dimples in both cheeks. She was timid and asked me for a biscuit and a glass of water. I made no promises as to the biscuit but fortunately was able to ensure that she had some water. Her father popped out of the court, leaving her with me, and returned with a range of chocolate bars. She grabbed the one closest to her and ripped the wrapper open. She demolished the bar within seconds and then sat there licking the crumbs from her fingers. Her childish mannerisms were endearing. She wasn't the terrified young teenager that I was expecting to see.

Sarah accepted what she did was wrong and she told me that she planned to plead guilty. But once her dad realised that she wanted to plead guilty he threw his chair across the room and screamed that we had all wasted his time as he had to miss work to attend court. He stormed out of the court building, leaving his worried daughter in a conference room with me. Sarah said that her dad was always like that and she had become used to it. I worried that a child had to regularly witness outbreaks of violence from her caregiver and saw a clear link between her behaviour and her experiences at home.

Sarah had no previous convictions and I successfully argued that the case should be sent back to the police for them to deal with outside of the courtroom. The most likely outcome would be that she would receive a youth caution (from the police) but it was clear to me that this case did not belong in court.

The issues we see in the adult courts are magnified in the youth courts. There are young people suffering with mental health concerns and learning difficulties. Many children are experiencing domestic violence, particularly at the hands of family members with alcohol or drug addictions. A Ministry of Justice study in 2012 found that

29 per cent of adult prisoners surveyed had experienced abuse and 41 per cent had seen domestic violence in their homes in their childhood, which was particularly prevalent in households where a family member had an alcohol or drug problem.[4]

Our training as barristers doesn't cover every skill we need to be able to deal with all of the difficult problems in our clients' lives. We rarely have time to process how our cases affect us because the next day it's another client and another problem. It took some time for me to learn to draw a line under a case at the end of each day. I always knew it was something I'd have to do but it was more difficult than I expected; my clients are real people and, at first, I couldn't easily switch off. I don't think I ever stop caring about my clients, even once the case ends, but after a few months I realised that I had to stop thinking about the client once the case ended and focus on the next case.

---

[4] 'Prisoners' childhood and family backgrounds: Results from the Surveying Prisoner Crime Reduction (SPCR) longitudinal cohort study of prisoners', Ministry of Justice, March 2012. https://assets.publishing.service.gov.uk/government/uploads/system/uploads/attachment_data/file/278837/prisoners-childhood-family-backgrounds.pdf

10

Protecting the Vulnerable

Youths aren't the only vulnerable people in the criminal justice system. Mr Barry was a middle-aged white man who was appearing in court for his sentencing hearing. He had been convicted in his absence. He had not attended his trial because he had been homeless at the time and could not afford travel to the court. He was now able to attend the sentencing hearing with the assistance of his new key worker.

Mr Barry was charged with an assault by battery. The incident had taken place at a supported home where Mr Barry was living. The home provided support for adults with mental health illnesses who needed assistance with day-to-day living. Mr Barry had been diagnosed with paranoid schizophrenia. He had been admitted to mental health hospitals on a number of occasions in the past. On the day in question, he had become angry with another person living in the home and they engaged in a verbal argument. A support worker intervened and Mr Barry had pushed him away. As a consequence of being charged with this offence, Mr Barry had been evicted from the supported home, which is how he had ended up homeless.

When Mr Barry arrived, he was friendly but agitated. He was sweating profusely and found it difficult to sit down. I spoke to the probation services and they helped me to contact the mental health team who came to consult Mr Barry. The probation officer then interviewed him in order to give an oral report on an appropriate sentence.

Eventually, the case was called. I explained to the court how difficult the circumstances were in this case. Mr Barry had been living in a supported home, which specifically catered for people with mental health illnesses. Whilst his actions were clearly wrong, his condition may have influenced his behaviour.

The mental health team supported that conclusion and explained that his paranoid schizophrenia was both chronic and enduring. The probation officer recommended a community order with a Rehabilitation Activity Requirement (RAR). Mr Barry would have to attend specific activities, for example anger management sessions, to address his offending behaviour. I argued that imposing too many requirements might be setting Mr Barry up to fail given that he had just managed to get himself somewhere to stay.

Thankfully, the court agreed with me. The magistrates read out Mr Barry's sentence, whilst he twitched nervously in the dock. 'Mr Barry, we have listened very carefully to what everyone has had to say about you.'

Mr Barry politely nodded and said, 'Yes sir'.

'We have thought long and hard. We have decided that this is one of those cases where a punishment would be irrelevant. Mr Barry, we are going to give you a conditional discharge of 12 months. We won't make any order for costs but you must pay a £20 victim surcharge, which everyone has to pay.'

He nodded and said that he only had £2.57 on him but could pay when his benefits came in. He was given a month to pay.

Although this case felt like it should never have been in court, this was certainly the right result. The criminal justice system is overloaded with vulnerable people and so many of them are not able to access the support and assistance that they need. In law, those defined as vulnerable witnesses (which includes defendants)[1] includes children (defined as people under the age of 18); anyone suffering from a mental disorder (defined by the Mental Health Act); anyone whose intelligence and social functioning is significantly impaired and anyone with a physical disability or who suffers from a physical disorder.[2]

---

[1] Defendants giving evidence at their own trial are 'defence witnesses', in a similar way to how the complainant is a 'prosecution witness'. In addition, in multi-defendant trials, defendants who give evidence are witnesses in the other defendants' case (whether prosecution or defence witnesses).

[2] Defined by section 16 Youth Justice and Criminal Evidence Act 1999 (YJCEA).

More than one-third of the average monthly prison population reports having mental health or well-being issues at any one time.[3] It's a devastating cycle for many people who are caught up in the criminal justice system and who will struggle to make their way out of this damaging cycle without significant intervention and long-term support.

Many of my clients are vulnerable in some way. Some of my clients have diagnosed mental or physical health issues but others have undiagnosed issues that only come to light once they enter the court system. In both my criminal and family law cases, I see instances of abuse. Many individuals who end up in court have been, or currently are, in local authority care. I've had clients who cannot read and many who have difficulties with speech and language. During pupillage I dealt with clients who were deemed by the Home Office to be victims of modern slavery or child exploitation, like my youth court client Layla.

I often meet a vulnerable client for the first time at court and then may never see them again. Some have a lasting impact. One of the hardest things about my job is not knowing how things turned out. As junior barristers we largely cover other people's cases and so we slot into the

---

[3] 37 per cent of prisoners, HM Inspectorate of Prisons surveys, the National Audit Office statistics https://www.nao.org.uk/wp-content/uploads/2017/06/Mental-health-in-prisons.pdf

gaps that need filling. We have to trust that other people will continue to support these vulnerable clients.

The criminal justice system has a long way to go before it can be said to adequately cater to those suffering from serious mental health issues. However, for people who are found to be guilty of an offence but who need professional medical help, there are some options. In some circumstances, the court can issue an order to send a person to hospital instead of prison. This is known as a 'hospital order' and can be made in the Magistrates' Court or the Crown Court.

There are a number of conditions that have to apply in order for someone to be eligible for a hospital order. Firstly, the defendant must have been convicted of an offence that could result in a prison sentence. The second condition is that two doctors must give evidence that the defendant has a mental disorder that means that they should be in hospital for treatment, and the appropriate treatment must be available. The court must then decide that a hospital order is the most suitable method of dealing with the case. I have represented clients in cases where hospital orders appear to be the only viable way of dealing with the case.

I prosecuted Mr Stroud's case in the Crown Court. Mr Stroud had pleaded guilty to a number of sexual offences including sexual communication with a child and breaching his Sexual Harm Prevention Order by having unsupervised contact with a child.

A number of my friends had asked me how I would feel *defending* an alleged sex offender, particularly a defendant who was charged with sexual offences against a child. Prior to prosecuting Mr Stroud, I had defended alleged and convicted sex offenders. Admittedly, I had been anxious when I had first received case papers to represent a sex offender for the first time at his parole hearing. That client was already serving time in prison for offences against children that he had pleaded guilty for. The offences were so serious that my client had changed his name to protect his identity.

I had read about these sorts of offences in the news and had studied them at law school but nothing could prepare me for representing a client already convicted of these crimes. For the first time I worried about the impact of my work. How would I feel if, due to my hard work, he was released and then reoffended? I felt torn but I knew that I had a duty to best represent his interests. I prepared the case meticulously and tried to focus on the law to distract myself from my personal views on the alleged offence.

When I entered the prison conference room to have a meeting with that first client, my nerves slipped away. Just like many of my other clients, he was trusting me with his liberty and it was my duty to do the best possible job. Everyone deserves representation and it's important that every individual in our justice system has access to a legal representative who will act in their best interests. At Mr Stroud's sentencing hearing he was escorted to court by a team of medical professionals as he was already an in-patient at a specialist mental health hospital. He was a fairly young man, which surprised me given his extensive list of previous convictions. The judge asked him to identify himself and then he was told to take a seat in the dock. He seemed to be heavily medicated as his movements were slow and clumsy. He stared into the space in front of him.

I outlined the charges and described the facts to the court. Mr Stroud had made sexual comments to a child that he did not know. I flagged to the judge that he had a long history of similar offences. The parents of the child had written a statement to the court, expressing how distressed their child had felt since the incident.

A doctor from the hospital attended court to give evidence about Mr Stroud's mental health. The judge asked the doctor a number of questions. During questioning, the doctor informed the court that Mr Stroud exhibited some symptoms of schizophrenia and was currently taking anti-psychotic medication, which seemed to explain his demeanour. Unsurprisingly, the doctor suggested to the judge that a hospital order would be suitable for Mr Stroud. He said that he felt it would help him in the long term and was an appropriate safeguard to protect the public.

The judge asked whether there were any beds available at the hospital. The doctor smiled kindly: 'Yes, there is a bed available; he already has one.'

The judge nodded and made a note.

For a client to be sentenced to a hospital order, arrangements must be made for the defendant to go to hospital within 28 days of the order. In this case, because the defendant already had a bed at the hospital there was no issue. However, in my first six months as a pupil, I observed cases where there were no beds available and so a hospital order could not be made. When this happens the case may be adjourned until a bed becomes available. In the meantime, a defendant may have to wait in prison if they aren't granted bail. In one reported case, the hearing was adjourned numerous times and no bed became available so the judge felt he had no choice but to pass a custodial sentence for public protection.[4] Someone who doctors believed – and a judge had agreed – should be in hospital was sent to prison. This shows the harsh reality of underfunding in the criminal justice system and the detrimental effect it can have on vulnerable people.

Mr Stroud sat in silence throughout his hearing. He was asked to stand up as the judge announced that he agreed with the doctor's recommendations. Mr Stroud

---

[4] This case is *R v Matthews* [2010] EWCA Crim 1936

was sentenced to a hospital order. Hospital orders initially last for six months but can be renewed by a responsible clinician[5] (usually a doctor) and there is no limit to the number of times it can be renewed. If it's not renewed, in most circumstances the defendant is free to leave the hospital if they wish.

Whilst the judge made clear that the hospital order replaced any prison sentence, he reminded Mr Stroud that the Sexual Harm Prevention Order continued to operate in the background. This meant that if he were to contact any child or otherwise breach the order in any way, he would commit an offence and he would be brought back to court.

I remember a unique case where even a hospital order was not thought to be appropriate. A young woman, Miss Lowe, had been drink driving and speeding. She had passengers in her car when she crashed into an oncoming vehicle. One of her passengers had died. Miss Lowe had suffered severe brain damage as a result of the accident. The brain damage was so serious that she now lived with a carer full-time. The judge had decided that Miss Lowe was not fit to plead.

There was a huge cry at the back of the courtroom as the family of the deceased passenger heard the judge's

---

[5] A 'responsible clinician' is the mental health professional in charge of a person's care and treatment while they are sectioned.

decision. The judge reminded the jury that two medical professionals had determined that Miss Lowe would not be able to understand the trial process and that she was not fit to stand trial.

When a defendant is deemed not fit to plead, there is no determination of whether the defendant is guilty or not guilty. Instead, the jury are just left to determine whether the defendant did the act that he or she was charged with. If the jury finds that they did, the court can make a hospital order, a supervision order (an order requiring a person to be under the supervision of a social worker or probation officer) or order an absolute discharge (the case is discharged with no further orders).

The jury found that Miss Lowe committed the act. In the circumstances, the judge deemed that a hospital order would not be appropriate in this case and Miss Lowe was discharged without further punishment.

A family member of the deceased passenger shouted out from the public gallery 'You are a killer! A killer!' at Miss Lowe, who seemed to have little awareness about what was going on. The family of the deceased were devastated. I remember seeing them sob hysterically in the courtroom. I could understand why they felt distressed. They felt that there was no justice as the person who had caused their son's death was facing no 'punishment'. However, I understood why the court had reached its decision: neither prison nor a hospital order would have achieved anything.

Miss Lowe and her father were taken to wait in a separate room for their own safety until the family of the deceased left the court building.

* * *

One of the most common 'special measures' in court is the use of separate waiting areas and screens. In criminal cases, prosecution witnesses are given a separate room to wait in and screens can be placed in the courtroom around a witness while they give their evidence. This is to avoid the defendant being able to see the witness or vice versa.

In family cases, separate waiting areas are often requested by solicitors but some courts don't have the facilities to ensure that this happens. Screens are used on a regular basis in court, particularly where a person has applied for a non-molestation order. A non-molestation order, put simply, is an order of the family court which aims to prevent a current or ex-partner, or another family member, from using or threatening violence, intimidation, harassment, pestering or otherwise harming the well-being of a person. It is similar to a restraining order but is ordered by the family courts against 'family members' (as defined by the Family Law Act).

A restraining order is usually put in place by the criminal courts when someone has been charged with an offence.

A criminal court can grant a restraining order regardless of whether the person is convicted of the offence; if a person is found not guilty, the prosecution may still be able to persuade the court that the complainant needs a restraining order for their protection. The main difference between the two orders is that a non-molestation order is granted in the family courts, whereas a restraining order is granted in the criminal courts.

Non-molestation order proceedings often begin with an emergency application without notice. The application is issued and heard by the court on the same day. One of my clients, Ms Mensah, had alleged that her ex-partner had raped her on numerous occasions and had been extremely violent; she showed me photos of the bruises all over her body. Whilst we were sitting in court, waiting for a judge to become available, I could see her phone ringing repeatedly. She became nervous and explained that it was her ex-partner checking up on her. She told me that he had called her multiple times in the half an hour we had been waiting. The reason she was making an emergency application without notice was because she was petrified of what he would do if he found out before she had the court's protection. If the court agreed to grant the order immediately without notice, he would only be told about the order once it was already in place and therefore would be in breach of a non-molestation order if he attempted a reprisal.

Ms Mensah was mostly concerned about her ex-partner harming her young child. This concern was what had made her seek help from the court. Just a few days ago, he had pushed her whilst she was carrying their baby. When the baby cried, he snatched the baby from her hands and shook him. Ms Mensah, through tears, told me that she had never been more scared in her life. Understandably, Ms Mensah asked me to make an application in court for her to have a separate waiting area and screens in the courtroom for the next hearing, which he would be attending.

In some cases, screens are properly requested but, due to miscommunication between legal representatives and the court, a screen is not put up on the day. This can be very distressing for a victim of domestic abuse who is terrified of seeing their ex-partner in court. On one occasion, my client was faced with the prospect of having to give evidence without a screen, despite the fact that her solicitor had applied for one. The suggestion was that my client proceed with the hearing without a screen or she would have to wait until the end of the day to be heard in an alternative courtroom.

It was understandably very upsetting for my client. She hadn't seen her ex-boyfriend since the last alleged violent incident. But as a single mother, she had childcare responsibilities that meant that she was not able to wait at court all day for a screen, even though the thought of seeing him frightened and intimidated her. In the end, she decided to go into the courtroom without a screen, but she was extremely uncomfortable and scared.

Another special measure that can be used is giving evidence by live link, like Ms Blackburn did because she was scared of Mr King in the first domestic abuse case I observed during my pupillage. In the youth courts, barristers also don't wear wigs and gowns and the barristers are supposed to remain seated, to try to make court feel less daunting for our young clients.

Whilst these special measures reduce the formality of the court and make the process less intimidating for vulnerable witnesses, they are not enforced with enough consistency. For example, despite all of the youth court guidance stating that barristers remain seated when talking to the court and asking the witnesses questions, I have been criticised by legal advisors, magistrates and judges for not standing in the youth court. If these special measures are to be taken seriously, they need to be consistently applied.

Giving evidence isn't easy and I gained a valuable insight into how much it can affect people whilst taking a weekend trip to the nail salon. I was chatting away to my nail therapist when I noticed that she seemed upset and distracted. I asked if everything was OK, which made her cry. She was appearing in court as a witness the following day and she was terrified of giving evidence. Her friend had been in a domestically abusive relationship and she had witnessed her friend's boyfriend physically attack her on multiple occasions. The abuse of her friend was ongoing, and she too had subsequently been attacked. Recently, she had tried to pull her friend's boyfriend off her friend as he was pulling out chunks of her hair. In response, her friend's boyfriend had bitten her. She pulled up her sleeve and I could still see the remnants of a nasty bruise.

I tried to comfort her, reassuring her that witness support services would be available to help her from the moment she stepped into court. They would be able to show her the courtroom before the trial and provide her with information about the court process. They would also be there to give her support on the day of the trial.

I felt obliged to ensure that this young woman understood how important it was for her to give honest evidence about what had happened and not allow her fears of repercussions to prevent that. Of course, it is much easier for me to say that when I am not the person who lives in close proximity to the defendant and is afraid of the possible consequence of giving evidence against someone who is violent. I tried to reassure her that the judge would be well acquainted with nervous witnesses and the court had a number of special measures that might help to put her at ease. She asked whether she would be able to go to the toilet if she needed to and whether the judge would be annoyed if she started crying. She explained that she suffered from anxiety and was terrified of the court process. The conversation made me realise that as barristers we should never take a witness giving evidence for granted. For many witnesses, it is the first time they have ever stepped foot in a courtroom and the experience is nerve-wracking.

* * *

Barristers have a huge responsibility. We bear a lot of that responsibility so early on in our career, without complaint. We are dealing with extremely vulnerable people when they are often at risk of losing their livelihood or freedom; or their children or family. These are typically the most important things to people.

Every day we witness a great deal of distress. The first time a client cried, my instant reaction was to reach into my bag for tissues and put my arm around his back. He had been accused of harassing his ex-girlfriend and was adamant that the communication had always been two-way. He showed me hundreds of text messages between them and was devastated that he was now appearing in court. He sobbed uncontrollably and I had to hold back my own tears.

It never gets easier watching people in their lowest moments. I try to not think about whether or not I believe a client because it doesn't matter. All that matters is that if they tell me that they are not guilty, I try my best to ensure that the court find them not guilty. Despite this, I did believe this client, and it was hard not to with the extensive two-way exchange in front of me.

I later represented this client at his trial and we won; the court found him not guilty. It was clear that the communication had been two-way and that my client had not been harassing his ex-girlfriend. I was delighted to have won his case, especially when I remembered how distressed he had been.

The criminal justice system is hard for the families of the accused too. One of the questions I'm most frequently asked by families is whether they can visit their loved one in custody in the cells, but the courts do not allow any social visits. It is tough. The court process is stressful and can cause everyone involved a huge amount of anxiety. I've comforted mothers, fathers, children, partners and friends outside courtrooms who are dealing with the wider consequences of their loved one being caught up in the criminal justice system.

I have no doubt that the court system is struggling to support vulnerable people. Whilst there are mechanisms for supporting witnesses and defendants, such as special measures, they are inconsistently applied. The victim support services provide excellent care for witnesses attending court but it relies on the goodwill of volunteers.

There is inadequate provision for defendants with mental health illnesses in the criminal justice system. Whilst hospital orders are possible, there are not sufficient resources in hospitals for defendants who need such orders to be granted. Similarly, many defendants with serious mental health illnesses are dragged through the court system, such as in cases like Mr Barry's where all he really needed was support.

I always strive for the best result for my vulnerable clients, which is challenging in this broken system. The pressure of attending court or being held in custody has a huge impact on defendants and their families and friends. I am the link between my client and the court and thus often have to deal with the stress and tension that arises, in the courtroom and outside it. If vulnerable people are to be properly protected there needs to be a much more unified application of special measures and more financial investment in the criminal justice system, particularly in relation to mental health.

11

Hoops and Hurdles

'There is no way he is seeing my son, no way!'

My client, Ms Walton, had only just walked into the conference room and tensions were already raised. She was shouting, despite me sitting less than one metre away. She pulled out the chair from underneath the table, further than it needed to be, and sat down stretching her legs out in front of her.

'I won't even consider it until we see those drug test results because I KNOW he is still smoking cannabis.'

It was obvious that the drug test results hadn't been shared with Ms Walton. I showed her the printed report, which confirmed that the hair strand testing for Mr Desmond, her ex-boyfriend, showed no trace of cannabis.

'Right,' she sighed. 'Well, he might have just stopped smoking the week before he took the test. What does this actually show?'

I explained to her that the report stated that the hair sample covered the past six months. She pulled her legs in and shuffled forwards on her chair to read the report herself. She glared at the page for a moment and then rocked back in her chair.

'I don't know what you want me to say.' Her voice was unsteady and I could see her lips trembling.

I tried to ease the tension in the room with a smile. I could tell this wasn't easy for her. Her son was only two years old and I could see that Ms Walton, a concerned mother, wanted to protect him. She tapped her phone screen to check the time and I saw that the background was a photo of her kissing her smiling son.

The statements that Ms Walton and Mr Desmond had written explained their background as a couple. They had been in a volatile relationship and both of them admitted that they had been physically violent to one another. That environment clearly was not conducive to raising a small child. They had separated just over a year ago and the child lived with Ms Walton. Since then, Mr Desmond had sporadic contact with the child until it stopped altogether a few months ago. They had now found themselves in the family court.

Ms Walton understood that Cafcass, the Children and Family Court Advisory and Support Service, would likely need to investigate and write a report, given the couple's history. These reports take a number of weeks and she was most concerned that in the meantime the court would order that Mr Desmond should have direct contact without sufficient safeguards. Mr Desmond currently only had indirect contact with his son: he sent birthday and Christmas cards and Ms Walton sent him photos and updates about their son.

Given her concerns (and the lack of neutral family members or friends who could assist with contact), the court was only likely to suggest direct contact in a contact centre, where it would be supervised or supported. Supervised contact is recommended when there is a risk to the physical safety or emotional well-being of a child; professionals oversee the session and can intervene if necessary. The parent is closely observed and there is a record of what happened. This was most appropriate for Mr Desmond. Supported contact is more appropriate where there are no concerns about the child's welfare, but the parents' relationship is such that a contact centre is the only neutral place for the child to see the other parent. Whilst there will be staff present in the contact centre, there will not necessarily be a member of staff in the room with the parent and child. In this scenario, the child isn't deemed to need protection from their parent so the staff present won't be observing the meeting and won't keep a written record of each session.

Ms Walton sighed. 'OK, yeah, if contact is supervised, that's fine.'

While Ms Walton went to get some fresh air, I

approached Mr Desmond, who was unrepresented. In the family courts the parties (or, if they have them, their legal representatives) are encouraged to speak before the hearing to see if any agreement can be reached outside of the courtroom. The legal representative might be a barrister at court or it can be the client's solicitor (either prior to the hearing or at the hearing if the solicitor is conducting the case without instructing a barrister).[1] Unfortunately, many people are unrepresented in family cases because legal aid is not available for most child arrangement order proceedings. There is a huge reliance on barristers acting pro bono. When that isn't an option either, people are forced to represent themselves. The courts are aware that this can create the perception of a power imbalance; judges and magistrates make an effort to ensure that everything is clear to the unrepresented party and I always try to explain as much as I can, whilst making it clear that I cannot provide them with any legal advice.

Mr Desmond wanted to see his son and he was frustrated that matters were being delayed further. He emphasised that he had done the hair strand test, as asked, and yet there

[1] In the family court, there are an increasing number of solicitors representing clients, usually for shorter hearings. This might be to save instructing a barrister or just because the solicitor chooses to do so. Solicitors can also take a Higher Rights of Audience course to be able to represent clients as a solicitor-advocate. With many solicitors advocating for their clients in court and barristers being permitted to conduct litigation (where they have applied to the Bar Standards Board to do so) there is less of a separation between the professions than has historically existed.

now seemed to be more hurdles for him to overcome. He was particularly worried about the possibility of Cafcass recommending a contact centre. He had looked into contact centres and said that he would not be able to afford to pay their sign-up fees, let alone their hourly rates.

Supervised contact in a contact centre can be very expensive. If ordered by the court, sometimes it will be free; however, if the parents have to pay, the fee can be in excess of £100 for a single session. Whilst contact centres are undoubtedly beneficial for many parents who might otherwise be unable to see their children, the cost of using them can put people under considerable financial strain.

'So, will I be able to see my son from today?' Mr Desmond looked at me hopefully.

I explained that Ms Walton would only agree to supervised sessions in a contact centre at this stage. His face reddened and I could see him press his lips firmly together. His eyes bulged and he lowered his brows into a scowl. He asked, 'Supervised? With what money?'

I apologised that I wasn't able to provide him with any advice as I represented Ms Walton. He shook his head in disbelief. I stood up and headed back to Ms Walton in the conference room. The usher stopped me just before I got to the door and said that the court was ready.

As Mr Desmond had applied for access to his child, he was addressed first.

Mr Desmond sat up in his chair and tugged at his tie, which appeared to be suffocating him. He took a deep breath and began: 'Ms Walton has alienated me from my son. She has taken my son away from me and—'

The magistrates stopped him and asked him to focus on the issues for the hearing. 'Mr Desmond, do you think that it might be sensible for Cafcass to speak to you both and write a report? They are a neutral third party and can help us make the right decision.'

I could see from Mr Desmond's expression that he was becoming increasingly irritated. He replied that he didn't want there to be any further delays to him seeing his son. The magistrates listened and made some notes as he spoke. Without replying to what he had said, they asked whether he had any proposals for interim contact.

Mr Desmond's scowl faded and he opened his notepad to read from the notes he had prepared. He detailed to the magistrates the days he would like to see his son and on which nights he would like his son to stay overnight. The magistrates stopped him again and asked whether he would be interested in supervised contact, in a contact centre, at this point.

Mr Desmond looked at me out of the corner of his eye. The room could feel his hesitation. Reluctantly he said: 'If that's the only option, then of course.'

Ms Walton let out a sigh of relief but it was premature. Mr

Desmond spoke again: 'But, if I have to have supervised contact in a contact centre, then I want her to pay half of the costs.'

The Chair of the magistrates then turned to me and asked what Ms Walton's position was, given the drug test results. I agreed that a report from Cafcass would be helpful as Ms Walton had ongoing concerns about Mr Desmond's ability to care for their son.

The Chair of the magistrates interrupted me. 'Yes, Ms Wilson, thank you. We have noted Ms Walton's apprehensions. It seems that a report from Cafcass is the only sensible way forward.'

I nodded and the magistrates continued. 'Ms Wilson, what about interim contact? What is Ms Walton's position on that?'

'Ms Walton is content for Mr Desmond to have supervised contact in a contact centre. But Ms Walton cannot afford to pay half of the costs of a contact centre.' I explained that she was unemployed, on benefits and the sole financial provider for the child. Mr Desmond, on the other hand, had a job and currently made no financial contribution to the raising of their child.

The magistrates asked Mr Desmond whether it was true that he paid no maintenance.

'Yes, but only because I don't get to see my kid!'

The Chair of the magistrates looked unimpressed and

the magistrates all turned to each other and consulted in lowered voices. They paused their discussions and announced that they would leave the room to make their decision.

When they returned, the Chair of the magistrates stated their decision: 'We are not asking Ms Walton to make any financial contribution to the cost of a contact centre at this time, given her limited means.'

'That's not fair!' Mr Desmond shouted out.

'Mr Desmond. We gave you the opportunity to speak. You need to listen now.'

Mr Desmond sighed and tapped on the table as they concluded matters. As we were discharged from the courtroom he cursed under his breath.

A few months later, at the next hearing, I represented Ms Walton again. I had not received the report from Cafcass, which was supposed to have been given to the parties at least two weeks prior to this hearing. When I arrived at court, I spoke to the Cafcass officer who informed me that the report had not been completed; the person with responsibility for writing the report had moved jobs and somehow this report had been missed. This report was important and affected whether a father would see his son but it had somehow slipped through the cracks. I could see why people felt that the system was broken.

Ms Walton arrived at court and explained that Mr

Desmond had not seen their child as he maintained that he could not afford to pay for the supervised contact. Mr Desmond was irritable and refused to speak to me. He asked to see the Cafcass report and was understandably upset that it had not been completed.

The court hearing was over quickly. The magistrates adjourned the case and directed that Cafcass complete the report in a timely manner. The court didn't have any availability for a number of months. Frustrated, Mr Desmond stormed out of the court building.

The third time I represented Ms Walton, almost eight months after I had first represented her, there was finally some progress. Cafcass had completed their report. They recommended that direct contact begin, supervised to begin with but progressing to unsupervised after just two sessions.

Mr Desmond, exhausted by the process and gutted to still not have seen his child, was happy with this. Ms Walton was nervous but agreed that things needed to progress.

A final order (meaning that they did not have to come back to court for further orders) was made, by consent. They agreed that Mr Desmond would pay for two supervised sessions in their local contact centre and thereafter would spend alternating Saturday or Sunday daytimes with their child, out in the community. They had agreed this via me, running backwards and forwards between them, before we were called into their final court hearing.

There was a positive ending to Ms Walton's and Mr Desmond's case in that their child would now benefit from having a relationship with both parents. However, the burdened court system delayed Mr Desmond rebuilding a bond with his child. It doesn't help that many individuals are forced to navigate the family courts alone because they are unrepresented and do not have the benefit of someone being able to advise them. Of course, the court's primary concern is safeguarding children but the delay and expense can make reaching a long-term solution very challenging for many families.

* * *

I was getting closer to thinking about life after pupillage. The tenancy decision was just over one month away and I had started to feel exhausted all of the time. I worried about what was going to happen at the end of my 12-month pupillage. If I wasn't successful in my tenancy application, I would have to apply for a third six-month pupillage at another chambers. I knew that my instructing solicitors would be writing references for me and I hoped that all of the feedback from clients had been positive.

There was one client who I knew was unhappy, Mr Cruz. Another country was alleging that he had fled the jurisdiction after being convicted of an armed robbery and rape and the UK courts were reluctant to grant him bail whilst determining whether he would be extradited.

He had made two bail applications – the maximum allowed – both of which failed and there had been no change in his circumstances to justify a further application. He said he wanted to be temporarily released on bail to sort out finances for his family. I explained that he was not allowed to make another bail application and he threatened to make a complaint against me if I did not make one. He repeatedly shouted at me, 'You work for me, remember!'

I was especially worried about him making a complaint, although I knew it would be entirely unjustified. I called a colleague and triple checked that, based on what my client had told me, there were no grounds for making another application and she reassured me that I was right to say no. But I was too scared to confess to her or anyone else at chambers that the client had threatened to make a complaint. I didn't even want the word 'complaint' to be associated with me. I overthought the situation and imagined someone mishearing that I had a complaint and then voting against me in the tenancy decision. This was the definition of pupillage paranoia. (Despite my fears, Mr Cruz never actually complained.)

Thankfully most of my clients asked their solicitors whether I could represent them again and I had by now taken on enough cases of my own to have some repeat clients. Though for obvious reasons this wasn't always necessarily a good thing. I had represented one client, Ms Crow, in a burglary trial, which we had won. She was now back in court for another burglary and had asked that I represent her. I was flattered but saddened to see that she was in court again. My instructing solicitors told me that they had known Ms Crow since she was a teenager and had represented her throughout her life. I thought about some of the young people I have represented and how heartbreaking it would be to see them in court in 30 or 40 years.

Ms Crow had more previous convictions than any client I had represented. Her first conviction, at just 11 years old, was for theft. She was now almost 50 and her previous convictions painted a picture of someone who was trapped in the criminal justice system. The only gaps in her offending history were whilst she was serving time in prison. Most of her previous offences were thefts and burglaries and she had engaged in some low-level fraud.

She had been remanded in custody for this alleged burglary but hadn't arrived on the prison transport vehicle with everyone else from that prison. After numerous enquiries, the cell staff told me that she was coming in a separate vehicle because she said her leg was injured and she couldn't walk properly.

When she eventually arrived at court, she told me that she was pleading not guilty to the burglary and needed to be out of prison. Her instructions were straightforward. I warned her that the sentencing guidelines recommended a significant custodial sentence and credit received for pleading guilty would make a big difference in this case.

She replied, 'Look, Alex, I picked you. I've had a lot of barristers. I feel like you can get me out of here today.'

I swallowed hard. I wasn't a miracle worker and I had to manage her expectations. Whilst there was a possibility she would be leaving today, it was more likely that she would remain in custody. She wasn't listening and I felt the pressure increase.

We patiently waited for the court staff to help Ms Crow upstairs into the dock. She sighed and yelped as she sat down, emphasising the pain that she was in. The judge waited until she was comfortable and then began. Ms Crow entered her not guilty plea and the prosecutor told the judge about the facts. Ms Crow was said to have taken jewellery from a number of houses in the same street. The prosecution was relying on a CCTV still, which they claimed was obviously her. The image was blurry and the judge didn't need me to point out that the most you could see was that the offender was a white woman with dark hair.

Thankfully, the judge agreed to grant her bail. She was going to be released until her trial date.

I headed down to the court cells. Ms Crow was ready to leave and I asked if she needed assistance getting back upstairs.

'Why would I need help?' she asked.

I looked at her confused.

She shook each leg and hopped from one leg to the other. 'Freedom is a healer,' she smirked and headed towards the door. She didn't even pretend to limp as she headed to the exit; she knew that the decision had been made and was keen to get away as quickly as possible.

I was in shock. I froze and watched her leave the building with a confident stride. Once she'd left it dawned on me how absurd that had been. I had no idea why she had pretended to be injured. I assumed she wanted some sympathy from the judge but it was a very unusual way to have gone about it.

* * *

After 11 months of attending court almost every working day, I was at least starting to feel like a 'real' barrister, even if I couldn't shake the anxiety about the upcoming tenancy decision. As with any job, many aspects of the profession that had felt strange or scary at the very beginning now seemed routine – standing up in court, being scanned by security when arriving at work each day, even putting on the wig and gown. But then one day at court something happened to make me reflect on it all anew.

I was sitting outside a courtroom waiting for a client who had not yet been brought to court by the prison when a young Asian male stormed out of the double doors towards me. He stopped directly in front of me.

'Are you a prosecutor?' he asked in a flat tone.

I confirmed that I was and asked if I could help.

'Fuck you! I hope one day you have to go to prison so you know what it's like. You lot have no idea.'

He stomped down the corridor kicking every door open and letting them slam behind him. The police and liaison officer had followed him out of court and had caught the end of our exchange. He reassured me that he would be speaking to the young man and asked if I was OK. I was a bit taken aback but I was fine. The officer explained that the man's brother had just been given a long prison sentence. I brushed it off and said that it didn't matter.

It was strange that my wig and gown had alienated me so much from this young man. I was seen as an enemy. I pulled the wig off of my head and sat there for a few minutes with it in my lap. Although I had always been so excited to wear my wig and gown, I felt an uncomfortable tightness in my chest. I caught my reflection in the mirror; this wig created a new identity for me. I thought back to the moment in the legal dress shop with my nan. My reflection looked so confident. My nan was proudly smiling behind me. My case was called and I put my wig back on and headed into court.

It was difficult to process the fact that my wig and gown had alienated me from someone. Thankfully, I was soon reminded that my personal experiences meant that I could relate more to some clients than others could.

It was 6.30pm and I had just got home from a long day at court. I stood in the kitchen preparing some dinner when I received a call from a solicitor asking whether I was free the following day to go to court the next day to represent her client. The client was upset with his previous barrister and at the last minute had said that he didn't want to be represented by him. She thought that I would be a 'good fit' for the client.

My client, Mr Hill, was a young mixed-race male who had pleaded guilty to possession with intent to supply class A drugs in the Crown Court. Today was just a mention hearing (an administrative hearing) to sort out the timetable for his confiscation proceedings. Confiscation proceedings happen after a defendant has been convicted of a crime where he or she has made a financial gain or has laundered criminal assets. The court will identify what the 'criminal benefit' was from the offending. In Mr Hill's case, the court were considering the profits from his drug dealing. This can be assessed in two ways. The simplest is when someone has benefited from a single crime. For example, if a defendant has made £1,000 by committing a fraud, his benefit from the 'particular criminal conduct' will be £1,000. The other way criminal benefit can be identified is from general criminal conduct. These are known as 'criminal lifestyle' cases. In these cases, the defendant is assumed to have financially benefitted from criminal activity over a six-year period unless he or she can show otherwise. The defendant has to prove that their financial gains in the past six years were not from criminal sources.

Drug dealing is an offence that can be treated as a 'criminal lifestyle' offence. I explained to Mr Hill that any unexplained income might be assumed to be a criminal benefit. His jaw dropped.

'So, you're telling me they are also going to take all my money?'

I paused momentarily. 'The court will try to recover what they see as your financial benefit from dealing drugs.'

'What the... I thought it would just be for the drugs they found on me. If I had known this...' he sighed and put his head in his hands. 'So, what, I go to prison and then I still have to pay all of this money?'

I nodded slowly. The prison sentence is the court's punishment; the confiscation is the recovery of financial benefit to stop people profiting from criminal activity.

Mr Hill leaned back against the wall of the cell. He

closed his eyes and took a deep breath.

'Yeah, it makes sense. Just, wow.'

I explained that they would assess the available amount. The court would make an order determining how much he would have to pay depending on how much he had available. They would look at his assets and his money. He looked startled.

'Do they know about my father's inheritance?'

I maintained eye contact and nodded. The police had found out that Mr Hill was due to receive some money from his father, who had recently passed away.

'So what am I supposed to do when I get out of here?'

I could see tears welling up in his eyes. I had no answer for him. The prosecution treated all of his money as 'available' for the purpose of confiscation, including legitimately received money. But this small inheritance might have given him the chance to stop selling drugs.

We finished our conference and I packed up my stuff. He was brought up from the cells into court and we agreed dates for him to provide information to the prosecution and for the prosecution to reply. There were several documents that needed to go back and forth between the defence and the prosecution. The next hearing wouldn't be for a few months.

I didn't see Mr Hill again because I worked tirelessly with his solicitor to ensure that the prosecution agreed a much lower figure than the one that they initially claimed Mr Hill owed. The proceedings came to an end without us needing to return to court for a contested hearing. Eventually we managed to agree an amount for Mr Hill to pay, which meant that some of his inheritance would be available for when he came out of prison.

I couldn't forget how shocked he was about the extent of the court's confiscation powers and wondered how many other people don't know what they are getting themselves into when they commit crimes.

A lack of understanding of the law and court procedures can cause all sorts of devastating consequences. For example, if a client doesn't understand a court order and this leads them to breach it then they can end up in even more trouble.

My client, Mr Lee, had breached a restraining order, imposed by the court, to protect his ex-wife, Mrs Lee. They had been married for over 20 years and the relationship had ended approximately a year before this case. The couple had four children together and both parents still played an active role in their children's lives.

The restraining order had come into place because Mrs Lee alleged that Mr Lee was harassing her constantly. She said that he refused to accept that the relationship was over and would turn up at the family home during the day and at night, begging her to take him back. After some time she stopped answering the door to him and she alleged that he became more and more frustrated to the point that he assaulted her in the street outside her house. She alleged that he had slapped her across the face, which he denied. Mr Lee was acquitted of the assault charge. I didn't represent Mr Lee in that trial and I didn't know what the evidence was but he maintained to me that he didn't hit her.

Despite Mr Lee's acquittal, the court imposed a restraining order. Courts have the power to make a restraining order even after acquitting a defendant if they deem it necessary to protect the complainant from harassment from the defendant.

In our conference, Mr Lee expressed how confused he still felt, despite the restraining order having been imposed months before. He didn't understand why he even had a restraining order, given that he had been found not guilty. I explained that the court has these powers to enable it to protect people in harassment cases where there is not enough evidence for the court to convict on the charges made but it is still clear to the court that the complainant needs the court's protection.

He was due to appear in court because he had been in phone contact with Mrs Lee and she had reported it to the police. He was extremely upset and kept repeating the same thing: 'But she has been calling me! Why is she not being charged?'

I explained again that the restraining order was against him, not her. I could understand his frustration and why he felt it was unfair.

'So what am I meant to do? Ignore her?'

I nodded. 'Yes, exactly. If she contacts you, you need to ignore her. The order is against you, Mr Lee.'

He asked how she would even prove that he had been the one calling her. He said he would just deny it; if she had recorded the calls that wouldn't show he called her. I pointed out that she had provided screenshots showing her call records and they showed the direction of the call. He tutted and rolled his head back.

'This is so ridiculous. This is so unfair. Screenshots?'

I showed him the screenshots of Mrs Lee's call list on my laptop. He complained that anyone could make up a screenshot and put a fake time there. I asked whether he wanted to challenge the legitimacy of the screenshots; he was adamant that he did.

I reflected on the fact that, as technology improves, our digital footprint makes it easier to prove or disprove that certain crimes have been committed. However, I was concerned by the lack of scrutiny in the way the courts treat this evidence. It was worrying that courts were willing to take screenshots of calls, messages and pictures at face value at a trial. Mr Lee was right – the call log could have easily been faked. Anyone could have called Mrs Lee and she might have just changed that contact in her phone to Mr Lee's name and it would look as though he had called her multiple times.

I had only received the screenshots the evening before the trial. There was no forensic testing of the phone. The phone was not available at court and so there was no opportunity to check the legitimacy of the call log screenshots.

So I tried to challenge the screenshot evidence, which had been provided by Mrs Lee. The prosecutor argued that if the defendant had wanted to challenge the screenshot evidence, he (or his solicitors) should have asked to examine the phone prior to the day of trial. I explained that I could not be responsible for what should have happened as I had only just been instructed in the case. I asked the court to either adjourn to enable these messages to be verified or exclude them on the basis of unfairness.

For his part, Mr Lee said that he didn't even know about the screenshots until the day of trial. He said that he hadn't had a conference with his solicitors and hadn't spoken to anyone about his case since his first appearance hearing. In the Magistrates' Court, there is rarely all of the evidence at the first appearance. The next (and only other) hearing is likely to be the trial date, by which time it is often too late for the defendant to challenge the evidence.

The application to adjourn the case was refused and

the screenshots remained. I was told that if the messages were disputed, I would have to cross-examine Mrs Lee about that, which is what I did. She denied falsifying the screenshots.

Mr Lee was found guilty after trial and was given a fine, reflecting that this was a minor breach and taking into consideration the fact that Mrs Lee had also been contacting him. He was irritated by the fine and told me that he understood that he wasn't to contact her again, but I wasn't convinced.

As we left court he turned to me and said, 'I don't know how you do this job. Court is bloody depressing.'

He was right, sometimes court can be depressing. As barristers, it's difficult when we lose a case and it is frustrating when we feel as though there has been injustice in the courtroom. It can feel that we are fighting for our clients in a broken justice system, rather than one that will ensure a fair result. The most that I can do is encourage my client to appeal the decision and hope that there is more procedural fairness the second time round when the appeal then goes to be heard in the Crown Court. Sometimes we are fighting an uphill battle and it can be difficult to stay optimistic. These challenges can be frustrating for both clients and barristers.

12

The Big Vote

'MS WILSON! DID I SAY YOU COULD LEAVE THE COURTROOM?'

The judge's voice echoed around the courtroom. I looked at her puzzled. I had just asked for extra time to have a conference with my client and she had agreed that I could have it. I had thanked her, stood up, lowered my head before turning my back and then slowly made my way to the door. I couldn't work out how she expected me to have a conference with my client – about footage from a police body camera that I had only just received from the prosecutor – without leaving the courtroom. There were recordings from two body-worn cameras being presented as evidence and my solicitors had received neither of them, yet the prosecution had claimed they had been sent. My client, Mr Wolff, was patiently waiting at the door of the courtroom.

'MS WILSON! YOU SHOULD HAVE BETTER MANNERS. YOU DO NOT LEAVE THE BENCH UNTIL I SAY SO. YOU ASK PERMISSION TO

STAND UP AND LEAVE. THIS IS NOT A FREE FOR ALL!'

Still confused, I muttered an apology to the judge. I then asked permission to leave and she nodded without looking up at me. I swiftly left the courtroom.

In 12 months of pupillage I had only been shouted at by a judge a handful of times, but every single time it upset me. This was my place of work, a professional environment, and I didn't expect to be shouted at whilst I was trying to do my job. But I was too exhausted to entertain this judge's criticism for even a second longer and I distracted myself by resuming the conference with my client.

Mr Wolff was charged with assaulting an emergency worker (a police officer). He had been stopped by an undercover police officer, in a park, and had struggled with the officer. The officer had emerged with a grazed knee and Mr Wolff was arrested. Mr Wolff explained to me that he was in an unfamiliar area and had been attacked in the past by other men because he used to hang around with some 'bad people'. He said that he had panicked when this man grabbed him out of the blue.

The officer claimed that he had reason to believe that Mr Wolff was selling drugs in the park and also that he was armed with a knife. There was a dispute as to when the officer had identified himself as a police officer. He claimed that he thought Mr Wolff would flee if he identified himself as an officer too soon and had grabbed him to prevent him escaping.

We watched the footage from the police officer's body camera. It was very unhelpful as it had been turned on a few minutes into the incident, when the struggle was already taking place, so the video had no context. Body-worn cameras are controlled by officers; they choose when to switch them on and off. The cameras automatically record a 30-second loop of film when they are in standby mode, so when a recording is started by the officer wearing the camera, the previous half a minute is always captured too, though without audio. The altercation had begun before this additional 30-second recording and so the extra silent footage added very little. Yet again, I was reminded that although technology has changed the nature of some evidence, it must be questioned and challenged in the same way as every other kind of evidence.

Body-worn video cameras were introduced as an independent witness to police actions and interactions. They are worn on an officer's chest and are intended to show the incident from the police officer's perspective. Importantly, the camera records the footage onto both an internal and secure storage device, and it is uploaded to secure infrastructure for use as evidence at court. So the problem with body-worn footage is not so much that it might be doctored or edited, but rather that the recording only begins when the officer chooses to start the recording, which can skew the context of the incident.

Having viewed the footage, Mr Wolff said that he was maintaining his not guilty plea.

When I returned to court the judge was perfectly pleasant to me. I told her my client was pleading not guilty and confirmed the names of the witnesses that we, the defence, wanted to cross-examine at trial. As with many of my cases, I didn't see this all the way through. At my level, it's unusual to represent the client from the first hearing to the end of the trial (especially if it goes to the Crown Court). This is because someone more senior is likely to be instructed for the Crown Court trial. Pupil barristers often won't find out what happened to a client they represented in the early stages of their case, which can be disappointing when you have put in a lot of hard work. In this case, I was particularly interested to see how the police officer would have been cross-examined about why he only turned his camera on after approaching Mr Wolff. If the officer wasn't able to properly explain his actions, his credibility may have been undermined in the jury's eyes. Body-worn video camera footage is only credible if it records the incident in its entirety. My limited involvement in this case had shown me that incomplete footage might be enough for the jury to be unsure of a person's guilt and hence acquit a defendant.

It was less than a month until my tenancy decision and to my other worries I added my concern that this judge would report back to my chambers that I had tried to leave the courtroom without asking for her express permission. Or, worse still, would my client tell my instructing solicitor that I had upset the judge to the point of her shouting at me? It is hard to remember not to take it personally when someone loses their temper in court. Courts are stressful at the best of times for everyone in the process. Judges are overworked, as are many barristers and solicitors. More importantly, though, courts are most stressful for those whose case it is.

* * *

Whilst my tenancy decision felt like the most important factor affecting my life, I knew that there were far more important decisions affecting my clients' lives. I represented a man, Mr Goffman, who was being held in custody on remand. He was alleged to have been domestically abusive. Unusually, the complainant, Ms Kaur, was not a partner or a family member; she was a 'friend' that he occasionally had a sexual encounter with.

The incident had occurred late at night, when he had visited her house to have drinks. They had been drinking alcohol and had a heated argument about a text message from another man. The message was allegedly sexually suggestive and Mr Goffman felt that she was making a fool of him. Mr Goffman and Ms Kaur seemed to agree that they were arguing about whether he had a right to be angry, given that they were not in a relationship, but they disagreed about what happened following that.

Ms Kaur said he lashed out, pushing her off a chair and kicking her. Mr Goffman said that she hit him because he said spiteful things, in retaliation to hearing that she was seeing other people, and that the most he did was push her off of him in self-defence. The court had refused two applications for him to be granted bail on the grounds that they believed he would intimidate Ms Kaur.

Since his bail had been refused, he had spent the past two months in prison awaiting his trial and had reached the custody time limit (the maximum amount of time he could be kept in prison without being convicted) for his offences. This meant that he could not be held in custody any longer without the court giving permission for the time limit to be extended. If his trial was adjourned and an extension was not granted, he would have to be released pending his trial.

Custody time limits are 56 days for summary only offences (the most minor offences, which can only be tried in the Magistrates' Court). For either-way offences (offences that can be tried in the Magistrates' Court or the Crown Court), the time limit is 70 days but the CPS try to ensure that the trial happens within 56 days. If a case is sent to the Crown Court for trial,[1] or if the defendant chooses to have a Crown Court trial (which a defendant can do if it is an either-way offence), or if it's an indictable offence (that must be tried in the Crown Court) the custody time limit is 182 days.

Mr Goffman's case was still in the Magistrates' Court and his two months were up. Ms Kaur gave evidence in court behind a screen and I cross-examined her about the incident that night. Mr Goffman also gave evidence about what had happened that evening. The district judge determining this case did not leave the courtroom to consider his decision. Seconds after hearing my closing remarks, he told Mr Goffman that he could not be sure that he had committed the offence alleged and hence was found not guilty. Mr Goffman and his parents, who had attended court to support him, were delighted that he was finally released but also, quite understandably, frustrated. Mr Goffman had been held in custody for two months without being convicted of any offence. He knew that he had lost his job and, given that he lived in a house rented from the council, he was worried that he might have lost his accommodation too.

I went down to the court cells after our conference.

---

[1] If it is an either-way offence that the Magistrates' Court feel is too serious it will be sent to the Crown Court. An indictable only offence will automatically go straight to the Crown Court.

He thanked me for my help and said he was glad I had represented him. He sat still for a moment, staring into his hands. Lifting his head solemnly, he asked: 'How do I get compensation for this?'

It felt like there was no air in the small, grotty cell. I could see that he was pleased with the outcome of this trial but I understood why he was upset. Unfortunately there is no compensation for those who are held on remand and found not guilty, or who have the charges against them dropped. Many defendants whose cases are in the Crown Court are kept in prison for up to six months (and sometimes longer if the limit is extended), without being convicted of an offence. Many of my clients who are stripped of their freedom whilst awaiting trial feel as though it undermines the principle that they are 'innocent until proven guilty'.

The justification for remanding people in custody is that the court has to find a way to ensure that complainants and the general public are protected. Serious trials can take months of preparation and, in some cases, there might be a huge risk to the public in not keeping a person in custody during that period.

I explained to Mr Goffman that he wouldn't be receiving any compensation. His eyes welled up and I could see how hurt he was.

'I genuinely didn't do what she said, you know. My life

might be ruined. I should have just left as soon as I saw that text.'

Their argument had got out of control and had been a brutal lesson for Mr Goffman. In my head I agreed with him that he would have been better off if he had left, but voicing that opinion wouldn't help him feel any better. I understood how much prison broke families and relationships; I had seen how people struggled to regain employment and sort out their housing. I didn't have anything to add. I couldn't imagine how difficult it must have been for him over the past couple of months.

I sat in the cells comforting Mr Goffman as he cried.

* * *

The night before my tenancy decision I couldn't sleep. I had tried to distract myself all evening. My co-pupil and I had gone for dinner and the weather had been miserable and gloomy. We opted for a light dinner as we had both lost our appetite. I was grateful to have a co-pupil that I got along with as I had heard so many horror stories about pupil rivalry. At some chambers it is common for three or four pupils to be taken on, knowing that only one or two are offered tenancy. This can create a hostile atmosphere among pupils who may feel that they have to upstage one another in competing for a permanent place in chambers. At my chambers we were told that there was space for us both to be taken on as tenants, providing we both proved to be good enough. We were lucky to have been encouraged from the beginning of our pupillage to work together rather than against each other. It really helped now more than ever. We were both incredibly anxious and it was comforting to have someone who understood what I was going through.

It felt like the most important 'results day' yet. Since finishing school at 18, I had completed a three-year undergraduate degree; a one-year postgraduate diploma in law; a one-year combined master's degree and Bar Professional Training Course and a year of pupillage training. Six years after finishing my A levels, I had the same nervousness that I'd had as a teenager waiting to see if I'd be going to the University of Oxford. My anxiety was through the roof.

Every time I allowed myself to slip into sleep, I would dream that the news was negative and I woke up sweating. I knew I was placing too much on this one decision. Many of the most successful barristers were not taken on first time and were asked to do a third six-month pupillage elsewhere, but that didn't calm my nerves.

We were told that we would receive a call in the morning once the chambers' AGM started at 10am. From 10am on the dot, my co-pupil and I were messaging each other every second to see whether the other had heard anything.

We were too scared to even use the bathroom in case that was when the all-important call came through. I tried to distract myself in every way possible but nothing worked. I warned my family to stay away and I buried myself under my duvet, refusing to get up until I received the call.

My phone started to ring and I saw that it was my first supervisor. My heart began to beat faster and with a shaking hand I answered the call.

'Congratulations Alex.'

I didn't hear anything after this, I just kept asking my supervisor whether he was joking. I could not believe my ears. Had I really made it this far? I kept thinking: I am a barrister; not a pupil barrister, but a fully qualified barrister.

Like an excited child on Christmas morning, I jumped out of bed and raced down the stairs. My parents and my siblings were waiting in the hallway and the huge smile on my face gave away the result – we all screamed in unison. They gave me congratulation cards that they had already written out and we laughed at how awkward this could have been. My mum went to the fridge and retrieved a cold bottle of champagne. My sister excitedly opened it, nearly taking my eye out with the cork! We poured our bubbles and I held them all in a long hug. Family got me through the experience and I couldn't have been more grateful for their love and support.

Thankfully my co-pupil had been offered tenancy too. We were invited to join everyone in chambers in the pub for a drink before going out for a big lunch. It was so nice to see so many members of chambers together and everyone was congratulatory. It was a good opportunity to finally relax around my colleagues. Many shared stories of when they got their tenancy. It seemed that every barrister went through the same paranoia.

On the first day in court after my tenancy decision I bounded into the court building. My hair was down and curly and the momentum of my stride made each of my curls bounce rhythmically. I wasn't adjusting my dress today – it looked fine and I knew it. The security guard greeted me with a smile. I sipped my drink before being asked to, unloaded my bag into the scanner and stepped on through. There was no beep today and I strolled over to collect my belongings.

In the advocates' room, I stood in front of the mirror grinning as I put on my court attire, tucking in my collarette bib and pulling on my gown. As I loosely tied up my hair, I was proud to see my defined curls at the bottom. I didn't need to glue my hair to my head. My hair is curly and that's who I am. Finally I lifted my wig and placed it down on my head. My reflection smiled back at me and I recalled a similar moment in that magical legal dress shop just over a year ago. A year had flown by.

I thought that becoming a tenant would change everything. I thought that pupillage was a means to an end. I couldn't have been more wrong. Of course, I had to do pupillage to become a tenant but pupillage was about so much more than that. Pupillage was a learning experience and probably the steepest learning curve that I have ever embarked upon.

* * *

Whilst accepting tenancy felt like a huge stepping stone, in reality it made very little difference to my daily work. On my first day as a tenant there was nothing setting me apart from any other pupil barrister, apart from a slight spring in my step. My client that morning, Toby, had no idea and probably couldn't have cared less, as he had more important things to worry about. He was a mixed-race, 13-year-old who was writing swear words on the wall of the waiting area as I tried to introduce myself. He completely ignored me. He had been in court a few times before and he was not fazed by the experience.

I was in the youth court representing Toby at his first appearance. He had been charged with a number of assaults against both his parents and a police officer who had been called to his home. Toby had behavioural difficulties and on the day in question he had lost his temper with his parents and started to smash things in the house.

His parents, trying to calm him down, had attempted to restrain him but he had lashed out at them too. His mother, feeling desperate, had called the police who arrived within minutes.

According to the police officer's statement, Toby had thrown an object at her forehead as soon as she stepped into the room. Toby shrugged when I read that part of the statement to him. I asked him whether he accepted that he did it, he smirked and said, 'Yeah, obviously.'

Toby turned his back to me and continued to etch words onto the wall of the waiting area. I read his most recent scrawl, which said 'fuck the feds'. I warned him that this was unlikely to help him in today's case but he shrugged again; the message wasn't getting through to him.

His parents had attended court to support him today but, because they were prosecution witnesses in this case, I couldn't speak to them. Toby's solicitor had told me that his parents had contacted him to tell him that they wanted to withdraw their statements. They said that they thought that they were obliged to provide statements to the police and they never intended for Toby to end up with criminal charges. Toby's solicitor had explained that he couldn't talk to his parents about it and suggested that they contact the CPS or speak to the CPS prosecutor at court.

At court, the prosecutor approached me to let me know that Toby's parents had spoken to her (and the police before attending court today) and that she was withdrawing the charges relating to them. Toby had one charge remaining: assaulting the police officer.

It was difficult to maintain conversation with Toby. Whilst he was polite to me, he had a short attention span and court was the last place he wanted to be. He was clear that he accepted assaulting the police officer and would plead guilty.

We were called into court and the legal advisor read the charge to Toby and asked for his plea. Toby shouted, in the loudest voice: 'Not guilty!'

This was, of course, not what we had discussed. I asked the magistrate whether I could speak to Toby. The magistrates turned to Toby and asked whether he had received legal advice, which he confirmed he had.

He declared, 'Just because I did it doesn't mean I have to plead guilty!'

The magistrates looked confused and tried to explain to Toby that if he pleaded not guilty then there will be a trial and a different, more serious, sentence may be given than they were willing to give today.

Toby's temper exploded. He stormed out of the courtroom swearing and kicking the furniture as he left. His parents chased him outside.

I left the courtroom and waited for Toby to return. When he eventually came back, we had another conversation in a private conference room. He was agitated but willing to speak to me. He just wanted the case to be over and he was finding the court environment difficult. I could understand his frustrations and explained his options: he could plead guilty and be sentenced today, or he could plead not guilty and a trial would be scheduled.

I had spoken to the youth offending team (YOT) officer who said that if he pleaded guilty, they would recommend that the court extend the referral order that he already had. A referral order is a community order for children (aged between 10 and 17 years old) that requires them to agree to a contract of rehabilitative work with the youth offending services. Since Toby had been in court before, he was already on a referral order. With no one else around he seemed to be listening to what I was saying. He looked up at me and stared for a moment, as if only just noticing that I was there.

We went back into court and Toby's parents sat silently at the back of the courtroom. He ignored them and walked to the chair next to me. The magistrates again asked him for his plea and he muttered that he wanted to plead guilty. The rest of the hearing was straightforward. As promised, the YOT officer recommended that the court extend his referral order and they did so.

Outside of court Toby disappeared into the bathroom, whilst his parents came to speak to me. His parents thanked me for my help and expressed how relieved they were that it was over. His mum cried and hugged me tightly. This case had been causing her so much anxiety and his parents had both been blaming themselves. They thanked me again and then stepped back to call their relatives and inform them of the outcome.

Toby reappeared from the bathroom and approached me. He looked up at me for the second time that day and whispered: 'Thanks.'

We made eye contact and I smiled. That small thank you meant a lot to me. I knew that Toby wouldn't have expressed gratitude unless he really meant it. It was clear that no one had told him to do so; his parents were in the corner still making calls. To me, his thank you meant that he knew that I was on his side. I was doing something right if Toby understood that I was there to help him and even thanked me for it. Toby half-smiled back and reluctantly went to wait beside his parents. That half-smile made my day.

* * *

A few days later I was back at the youth court. Joanna was very different from Toby. She was 15 years old and, unlike Toby, it was her first time in court. She was petite and had neatly combed hair, which she wore in a ponytail. She came to court in jeans and a pink jumper and sat quietly in the corner of the waiting area until I called out her name. Her mother had come with her to court. She was young and they could easily have been mistaken for sisters.

Joanna was charged with criminal damage for picking flowers from her neighbour's garden. Her mum explained to me that they had a difficult relationship with their neighbour. The neighbour was a complainer and would constantly find something new to object to. They had argued about parking, rubbish collection, postal delivery – everything and anything. On this occasion, the neighbour had moaned that Joanna's new cat was ruining their front garden.

At this point in the conversation Joanna spoke up. She told me how much she loved her new kitten and I could see the passion in her eyes. Her voice dropped when she told me that the neighbour had threatened to kill her kitten if he saw it in his front garden again. The threat of someone harming her kitten had upset her and she'd decided to teach her neighbour a lesson by plucking some of his flowers out of the ground.

To her credit, few of the flowers had been destroyed and her neighbour confirmed in his statement that he had been able to successfully replant most of them. However, he argued that the time and effort that it took him to repair his garden had been substantial. He reported it as a crime and that was why Joanna was in court.

As with some of the other youth court cases I had done, it was obvious that this case did not belong in court. I was fed up with seeing young people criminalised at such an early age. The consequences of a criminal conviction can be life-changing and it was worrying that so many minor cases were reaching court.

However, unlike in Sarah's case – the 13-year-old with learning difficulties who had smashed an interactive whiteboard at school – the youth offending team (YOT) officer did not support the notion that the case be sent back to the police for them to deal with it. This was the third time Joanna's case had been scheduled for a court hearing because she had not turned up to the previous hearings and the YOT were concerned. Joanna's mum admitted that the reason Joanna hadn't turned up for the previous hearings was entirely her fault, she had been busy and couldn't bring Joanna to court. The YOT officer, however, was not persuaded.

Despite my efforts, the court refused to adjourn for the police to consider an out of court disposal. This could mean no further action is taken, or a community resolution is decided upon – which might include an offer of compensation or an apology – or a youth caution is given (which can have conditions attached to it). The YOT officer did not support the recommendation and the prosecutor was adamant that the police had already considered it and had refused.

We were given a ten-minute break to discuss what Joanna wanted to do. The best option now was for Joanna to accept the criminal damage (which she did not dispute anyway) and receive a referral order. Joanna decided she would plead guilty.

We returned to court. The legal adviser read the charge to Joanna and asked how she wanted to plead, with no hesitation she said: 'Guilty.'

The prosecution then made an application for a restraining order, which I opposed. This case was not particularly serious and a restraining order could raise tensions between the neighbours. The court refused to grant a restraining order as they agreed with me that it was disproportionate. As expected, they gave Joanna a referral order.

In imposing her sentence the magistrates reprimanded her behaviour and I could see her rolling her eyes. The magistrates ignored it and I was grateful. It seemed to me like a nervous reaction. As we left the courtroom, Joanna was visibly upset. We sat in the waiting area outside the courtroom for a few moments whilst we waited for the YOT officer to come and talk to her about her referral order.

Unexpectedly, she turned to me and mumbled, 'Thanks, Alex.'

I smiled at her and reassured her that, providing she complied with her referral order, this was now the end of the matter.

Of the hundreds of cases I had taken on, this one challenged me in a different way. I had dealt with so many serious cases, where families had been broken, victims had been hurt and clients were at risk of losing their liberty, so it was frustrating that Joanna had been dragged into the criminal justice system, at such a young age, for something relatively minor. Her behaviour wasn't justified but it seemed unjust that she now had a criminal conviction on her record forever. For pulling up flowers.

* * *

Mr Owen had been charged with a public order offence for allegedly threatening a woman in public – in the language of the court he was said to have used 'threatening or abusive or insulting words or behaviour with intent to cause fear of or provoke unlawful violence'. The incident began as a disagreement over who would take a parking space. The complainant, Miss Cook, alleged that as she had tried to pull into a parking space, Mr Owen beeped repeatedly, undertook her and pulled into the space. She claimed that she could see him shouting obscenities at her, although her windows were up (and she was facing the opposite direction). She said that she swore back at him, which angered him so much that he got out of the car and grabbed her car door handle. She claimed she then drove off but he chased the car and kicked it repeatedly as she was driving off.

The CPS accepted that there was not enough evidence to charge Mr Owen with criminal damage (there was no damage to her car). However, they proceeded with the public order offence charge.

I represented Mr Owen at his trial. Mr Owen was a middle-aged, smartly dressed black man. He arrived at court early and we had plenty of time to talk through his case before the trial began. His instructions were clear, he parked up and got out of the car and was met with Miss Cook shouting abuse at him, including racial abuse. He told her to shut up and walked away. He didn't report it because he wasn't that bothered by the incident and said that he didn't trust that the police would do anything about it anyway. Unfortunately, although it had taken place in a public street, there were no witnesses to the incident.

Whilst we waited in court Mr Owen told me about his daughters. He was a family man. He had a picture of his wife and two children on his keyring and kept telling me that I reminded him of his oldest daughter, who was just 12 but wanted to be a lawyer. Mr Owen hoped to take his daughters to Disneyland Paris during the Christmas holidays and worried that if he was sent to prison he wouldn't be able to take them. I saw tears in his eyes as he told me how precious his children were to him and how frustrated he was that he had been made to come to court for something he didn't do. I tried to keep him focused on what had happened that day. I reassured him that although the maximum sentence was six months in prison, he was very unlikely to be facing a custodial sentence if he was convicted. The facts, as alleged by the complainant, would likely result in a fine or community order; particularly given that he had never been in trouble with the law before.

The prosecution made an application for Miss Cook to have a screen when giving her evidence, which I objected to. Miss Cook was not a vulnerable witness. She hadn't known Mr Owen prior to the incident and was unlikely to ever see him again, so there was no need for her to be shielded from him. The magistrates agreed with me and the application for a screen was refused.

I cross-examined Miss Cook on her account of what happened and her story changed drastically. She admitted the racial abuse but claimed that it followed Mr Cook racially abusing her, despite her not mentioning any of this in her witness statement. She also denied that she had ever said that he had kicked her car, despite this being in the witness statement that she confirmed that she read and signed.

Unsurprisingly, the magistrates did not find Miss Cook

to be a credible witness and they preferred Mr Owen's account. They found him not guilty.

As we stepped outside of the courtroom, Mr Owen embraced me in a huge bear hug. He pulled away and apologised but I smiled – I was so pleased for him. As I looked up at him, I could see tears of happiness rolling down his cheeks. He couldn't stop thanking me. We sat down in the waiting area as I packed my things into my bag and he told me how excited he was to take his children to Disneyland. Mr Owen said that he would value it more than anything now that he realised how quickly a person can lose everything. His smile grew and he announced: 'I can't wait to tell my daughters all about you.'

He started telling me how pleased he was to have been represented by a young black woman. His comments made my eyes well up. I could see the delight in his face. I had seen a similar expression in my own dad's face. I knew I had done a good job. I felt proud.

* * *

Even as I gain experience, this career remains emotionally challenging. It is impossible to completely detach myself from my work because I am involved in people's lives at some of their toughest moments and my representation can make a real difference. I take pride in the fact I am a barrister from a non-traditional background, my clients feel that I am relatable and trust me to help them with the significant choices they have to make. I often look back to the beginning of pupillage and smile at how far I've come. I used to question whether the Bar was for people like me, even whilst trying to prove it was. I wondered whether my race or my gender meant that I wasn't welcome, but I now know more than ever that the Bar needs people like me. The profession benefits from having and retaining women. It is essential that it embraces ethnic diversity too, especially given how overrepresented many ethnic minority groups are in the criminal justice system.

I also worried about my age. I knew I was young but it's proven to be an advantage. Some clients joke that I look younger than them (and I probably am) but it's made me more relatable to many of my clients than I could have even hoped. I was nervous that I would stick out at the Bar because I'm not posh, I don't come from an upper-class background. I realised it doesn't matter. If I am seen as different that can only be a good thing in a profession where we must represent all of society.

Now I am sure that the Bar is for people like me. I hope others who look like me, sound like me, or have a similar story to me, know that the Bar is for people like them. The Bar represents the whole of society; it should reflect that. I would like others to follow in my footsteps, just as I have followed in the footsteps of those who came before me.

Bibliography

I have included some of the books and reports that inspired me when writing this book, or that may be of interest to readers who enjoyed my book:

For more about institutional racism in the police in the UK: 'The Stephen Lawrence Inquiry: Report of an Inquiry' by Sir William Macpherson of Clunly https://assets.publishing.service.gov.uk/government/uploads/system/uploads/attachment_data/file/277111/4262.pdf

For a book about our broken justice system: Anonymous, *The Secret Barrister: Stories of the Law and How It's Broken*, Picador, 2018

For stories from an experienced family and criminal law barrister: Sarah Langford, *In Your Defence: Stories of Life and Law*, Doubleday, 2018

For discussions on how our justice system affects women:
Helena Kennedy, *Eve Was Shamed: How British Justice is Failing Women*, Chatto & Windus, 2018

For an insight into the criminal justice system in the US:
Michelle Alexander, *The New Jim Crow: Mass Incarceration in the Age of Colorblindness*, updated edition, The New Press, 2020

For insight into the wider role that race plays in society:
Yomi Adegoke and Elizabeth Uviebinené, *Slay in Your Lane: The Black Girl Bible*, Fourth Estate, 2018

Akala, *Natives: Race and Class in the Ruins of Empire*, Two Roads, 2018

Malorie Blackman, *Noughts and Crosses*, Simon & Schuster, 2005

Candice Carty-Williams, *Queenie*, Trapeze, 2019

Reni Eddo-Lodge, *Why I'm No Longer Talking to White People About Race*, Bloomsbury Circus, 2017

Michael Fuller, *Kill the Black One First: A Memoir*, Bonnier Books, 2019. Also available as *A Search for Belonging: A Story about Race, Identity, Belonging and Displacement*, Blink 535, 2020

Afua Hirsch, *Brit(ish): On Race, Identity and Belonging*, Jonathan Cape, 2018

Chelsea Kwakye and Ore Ogunbiyi, *Taking Up Space: The Black Girl's Manifesto for Change*, Merky Books, 2019

Trevor Noah, *Born a Crime: Stories from a South African Childhood*, John Murray, 2016

Michelle Obama, *Becoming*, Viking, 2018

David Olusoga, *Black and British: A Forgotten History*, Macmillan, 2016

Derek Owusu, *Safe: On Black British Men Reclaiming Space*, Trapeze, 2019

Layla F Saad, *Me and White Supremacy: How to Recognise Your Privilege, Combat Racism and Change the World*, Quercus, 2020

Nikesh Shukla, *The Good Immigrant*, Unbound, 2016

Angie Thomas, *The Hate U Give*, Balzer & Bray/Harperteen, 2017

Further Resources

There are numerous useful online resources on the law and justice system and the need for diversity.

The Inns of Court all have valuable resources:
  https://www.middletemple.org.uk/
  https://www.innertemple.org.uk/
  https://www.graysinn.org.uk/
  https://www.lincolnsinn.org.uk/

The Criminal Bar Association website:
  https://www.criminalbar.com/

The Family Law Bar Association:
  https://www.flba.co.uk/

The Bar Council have useful diversity projects including 'I am the Bar':
  https://www.barcouncil.org.uk/

The Bar Standards Board gives some of the crucial
   information about the profession:
   https://www.barstandardsboard.org.uk/

The Stephen Lawrence Trust:
   https://www.stephenlawrence.org.uk/

Just for Kids Law offers training and resources and
   videos for young people:
   https://justforkidslaw.org/

Acknowledgements

In no particular order, I would like to thank the following people.

Mum and Dad, thank you for never placing a ceiling on my achievements and for always encouraging me. You are my inspirations and this book wouldn't have been possible if it wasn't for your enthusiasm and support. My sister and my brothers, I love you three more than anything, thank you for letting me practise winning an argument long before becoming a barrister.

Nanny Jan, thank you for always being my cheerleader. I know you won't ever admit to having favourites but you are mine.

My grandparents, my cousins, my aunts and uncles, thank you all for your constant love and support.

My friends, you all know who you are. Thank you for being understanding and patient with me. Thanks you for always being at the end of the phone when I've needed you.

Thank you to everyone in my chambers. I am so lucky to have had the best supervisors during pupillage and to work somewhere where I can call my colleagues my

259

friends. And thank you to all of the wonderful barristers and judges at Middle Temple. Without my scholarship, I might not be at the Bar.

I also owe a huge thanks to my professional and lay clients. Thank you to all of my instructing solicitors for trusting me with our clients' cases. Thanks to all of my lay clients for also having faith in me on some of the most important days in their lives.

Hayley Steed, my wonderful agent. Thank you for having faith in me from the beginning of this journey. You aren't just my agent but also my friend. You are the best and we will forever be Essex sisters.

Claudia Connal, my editor, who has been exceptional. I cannot thank you enough for all of the work you have done with me on this book. Thank you for your patience and flexibility; working alongside a junior barrister with irregular hours is not easy!

Thank you to everyone at the Madeleine Milburn Agency for including me as part of the family.

Thank you to the fantastic people at Octopus Books, who have brought everything together. A particular thank you to Pauline Bache, my project editor; Jonathan Christie, Creative Director; and David Eldridge, who designed the wonderful cover (which I cried when I saw). Thank you to Victoria Scales and Karen

Baker, my publicists, for their amazing work during a global pandemic!

I am so grateful to you all.

Alex

About the Author

Alexandra Wilson is a junior barrister. She is the eldest of four children. Her mother is White British, her father is Black British and her paternal grandparents were born in Jamaica and came to England as part of the Windrush generation.

Alexandra grew up on the border of East London and Essex. She studied at the University of Oxford and was awarded two prestigious scholarships, enabling her to research the impact of police shootings in the US on young people's attitudes to the police. She went on to study for a Graduate Diploma in Law (GDL) and her Master of Laws at BPP University in London. Alexandra was awarded the first Queen's scholarship by the Honourable Society of the Middle Temple, a scholarship awarded to students showing exceptional promise in a career at the Bar.

Alongside her paid family and criminal law work, Alexandra helps to facilitate access to justice by providing legal representation for disenfranchised minorities and others on a pro-bono basis.

🐦 @EssexBarrister